WILDERNESS SURVIVAL

JAMES MOLENBEEK

WILDERNESS SURVIVAL

SUSTAINED FOR 40 DAYS IN FAITH, HOPE, AND LOVE

Wilderness Survival

Published in the United States by Credo House Publishers,
a division of Credo Communications, LLC, Grand Rapids, Michigan
credohousepublishers.com

ISBN: 978-1–62586-186-3

Cover and interior design by Sharon VanLoozenoord
Editing by Ann Byle

Printed in the United States of America

First edition

This book is dedicated to my wife Sue Anne,

my beloved partner in life and family,

my supporter and coworker in ministry.

THE WILDERNESS

Some places are so beautiful that words and pictures cannot adequately describe them. This is certainly true of Yosemite National Park in California, on the cover page, an iconic wilderness location. Thankfully there are beautiful places close to home and far away for short and long trips when we need to escape the regular routines and burdens of daily life. Our inner thirst is quenched by still waters.

Wilderness can restore us, yet life's wilderness places can make us feel threatened and lost. These experiences may be forty minutes of crisis, forty days of endurance, or forty years during which we need to be sustained. This book guides us into ways we can be sustained in such times with resources God provides. Trials come in many forms such as these listed here. This list isn't exhaustive.

Widow Widower Refugee Unemployed Exile RACISM

Deployed/Deployed Spouse Prejudice Cancer Divorce Downsized

Developmental Disability BUSINESS FAILURE Eligible for Hospice

Discrimination Bankrupt Low Vision *Dumped by boy/girlfriend*

POVERTY Quarantine Prodigal Son/Daughter/Grandchild

Mental Illness Betrayed Heart Attack *Lawsuit*

UNDER INVESTIGATION Suicide Convicted Felon LGBTQ+ Drought

Wounded Warrior *Mid-life Crisis* CHEMOTHERAPY Crippling Anxiety

Food Insecurity Covid-19 Co-morbidities Autism *Terminal Illness*

SEXUALLY HARASSED Chronic Illness Macular Problems Marital Affair

Deaf Obsolete Skillset Fire FRAMED Speech Impediment

Major Car Accident Flood Victim of Fraud PTSD *Evicted* BLIGHT

Crop Failure Tornado Fired SIDS Loss of child *Hungry*

MENTAL COLLAPSE Oppressed Amputation Incarcerated

Market Collapse Dementia Abandoned MISCARRIAGE Death of Parent

Loss of Friend Hurricane Job Offshored Automobile Injury

Termites ORGAN FAILURE Foreclosure Clinical Depression

Neurological Disease Estranged Family Learning Disability

Chronic Fatigue WITHERING CRITICISM Breakdown Lost Eviction

Chronic Anxiety Paralyzed *Shunned by Family* LOSS OF HEALTHCARE

Unsafe School Pervasive Sadness Deported Hunger Persecution

Moral Failure CHURCH CLOSURE Auto-immune Disease

Loss of Independence Driver's License Revocation

Failed a Class Out of Control Child *Victim of Injustice* DACA Home Invasion

Loved One in Prison Immigration Denied Banished Bullied

Friendless ILLEGAL ALIEN Hopeless Alcoholic Kidney Dialysis

Drug Addiction *Unemployed* FORCED RETIREMENT Drug Rehabilitation

Adultery Sub-Acute Rehab Primary Caregiver Overload

Radiation *Infertility* RAPE First Responder Unforgiven

Childhood Trauma Abortion Attachment Disorder *Failing*

HOW TO USE THIS BOOK

This devotional is designed for use by individuals, families, or small groups. It can be used during difficult seasons of life or seasons of the year such as Lent, and will add much to a personal or small group retreat. I encourage you to give it as a gift to someone in your life going through a wilderness experience.

Like many other devotionals, it includes Scripture, some commentary, and application. This 40-day devotional, a number rich in biblical symbolism, starts with two introductory devotions on Faith, Hope and Love, followed by twelve devotions each on Faith, then Hope, and finally Love. The final two devotions integrate these concepts.

My desire is not just to inform, but also to help you process the truths and your responses from different perspectives. To help, I have added visual, musical, and spiritual formation suggestions to integrate each day's thoughts more fully into your whole person. This will happen best when you put yourself into a meditative and worshipful spirit before the Lord.

SUGGESTIONS FOR USE:

1. Begin with a minute of quiet; de-clutter your mind to be more receptive. Slow deep breaths can help this transition.
2. Read the printed text. If you have a Bible handy, read the longer text suggested with each devotion to put the verse(s) in context. Scripture is from the New International Version (NIV), with an Appendix that lists the verse(s) in the King James Version (KJV).
3. Read the devotion thoughtfully.
4. Look at the visual following the devotion; consider what it says about the theme.
5. Look at the hymns suggested. If the words are in your memory bank, hum or sing them. If you have a hymnbook nearby, most will have at least one of the songs listed. Also consider playing a recording of one you like from an on-demand music streaming service.
6. Meditate reflectively alone or with your small group. Use the guiding questions if they are helpful to you.
7. Conclude with prayer, embracing the focus given each day and adding whatever is on your heart.
8. Read the Prayer of Blessing as the conclusion.

INVITATION TO READERS

© CANSTOCKPHOTO

We have been growing Morning Glories each summer longer than I can remember. I always plant the Heavenly Blue variety—because what other color should a pastor buy? I enjoy watching them unfold as the sunlight falls upon the blossoms, and the color is gorgeous.

The flowers remind me of how each day God's mercies unfold in our lives. God fed his people in the wilderness long ago with daily manna. Our Lord also taught us to pray, "Give us today our daily bread." We can continue to look for new manna and mercies each day.

This we also learn from Lamentations 3:19–23, words of encouragement out of a book filled with deep expressions of hurt and sorrow:

I remember my affliction and my wandering, the bitterness and the gall . . . and my soul is downcast within me. Yet this I call to mind and therefore I have hope. Because of the Lord's great love we are not consumed, for his compassions never fail. They are new every morning, great is your faithfulness.

This text underlies the beloved hymn *Great Is Thy Faithfulness* (text by Thomas O. Chisholm, tune by William M. Runyan, 1923).

Great is thy faithfulness! Great is thy faithfulness!
Morning by morning new mercies I see;
All I have needed thy hand hath provided.
Great is thy faithfulness, Lord, unto me!

May this be your experience every day. I pray that these 40 Days will refresh you.

DAY 1

THE DYNAMIC TRIO—FAITH, HOPE, AND LOVE

1 Corinthians 13:13 (read 1–13): And now these three remain: faith, hope, and love. But the greatest of these is love.

If you are familiar with the words *Faith, Hope,* and *Love* used together, it likely comes from this passage in the Bible. I have often read it at wedding ceremonies and used it in devotional messages around Valentine's Day. The words sound nice and warm, and all three are common in Christian vocabulary. But I hope to convince you and develop with you the awareness that these are not just "nice words." Rather, they convey essential truths from God that you need to live the Christian life and finish well.

Wherever you are on that journey, you will have times in the wilderness of life. Sometimes we seek wilderness places by choice because we love the solitude and wonder of escaping from the frenzied pace and pressures of modern life. We long for places where we can find renewal, where we can be restored by "quiet waters."

While it can be a great adventure, other forms of wilderness can seem like a bad dream that we cannot escape. Then it becomes a quest for survival in times of deep trial. We wonder, "How will I make it" or "Can I make it?" I have good news for you! We do make it through the wilderness with God's help and provision.

Key resources he provides are the lasting gifts of *faith, hope,* and *love.* We do not create them, though we have to develop and nurture each one for them to be effective. We must fully engage with them, receiving them as gifts from God that we must assemble and maintain over the course of a lifetime. This devotional guide will assist you in that glorious, difficult, worthwhile task.

God promises that his presence and grace will be with every Christian forever. He also provides the means through which our faith in him deepens, and our ability to look to the future in hope is sustained. All of which leads us to express love to him and embrace others with us on the journey through the wilderness. Think about it as being properly outfitted for a trip into the wilderness. Having the proper gear will determine if you will come back safely or need an emergency airlift.

Verse 13 (read it again above) speaks of faith, hope, and love as *remaining*, that is lasting all along our earthly journey. God will not cut off our supply. They will not expire before we do! We can, however, restrain their effects through spiritual apathy or willful neglect, but God wants us to enjoy their full use.

Stay close to Jesus Christ, the source of these gifts and all the blessings of his grace. I pray that you will discover the important place this dynamic trio has in your life, and through this book grow in your understanding and practical development of *faith, hope,* and *love.*

PSALMS, HYMNS, AND SONGS

Lead Me, Guide Me

Guide Me O Thou Great Jehovah

Day by Day

The Lord Leads the Way through the Wilderness

MEDITATION AND PRAYER

- What did I notice in particular about this reading?
- Did this bring to mind any recent experiences?
- Do I sense God prompting me to change or to do anything?
- I wonder . . .
- I thank God for . . .

PRAYER OF BLESSING

O God, source of every good and perfect gift, we give thanks for these gifts of faith, hope, and love working within us and through us. Help me to understand and develop them, to be upheld in the challenges of life. In Christ, amen.

Faith, Hope, and Love can be compared to the three primary colors; colors enrich our lives daily!

© ISTOCK

THANKSGIVING FOR FAITH, HOPE AND LOVE IN ACTION

Colossians 1:3–5: We always thank God, the Father of our Lord Jesus Christ, when we pray for you, because we have heard of your faith in Christ Jesus and of the love you have for all God's people—the faith and love that spring from the hope stored up for you in heaven and about which you have already heard in the true message of the gospel that has come to you.

Notice how one of the first things expressed in this passage is the important place of faith, hope, and love (true also in the beginning of 1 Thessalonians). These three stand out as key indicators to the apostle Paul that the Colossians were growing well as Christians. They were a small, emergent church in a religiously hostile world. As a community and individually, they faced constant challenge. Faith, hope, and love were constantly at work in the small church, which was cause for thanksgiving. The church was also noticed near and far, as Paul indicates.

Faith, hope, and love were indicators of success. They were central parts of Christian living for the Colossian church, and proved they had heard and accepted the Good News of Jesus Christ. What indicators do you use for success? How about your church? How we measure success is too often done in material terms and secular benchmarks.

This little church in Colossae had few members, many marginalized people, and no building. Yet they had the key signs of spiritual success. They heard the gospel and responded in faith. They belonged to Jesus, and the effects of belonging were working out in their lives and their community in tangible ways. They were authentic believers in an authentic church of Christ.

I will note throughout this study how you too need faith, hope, and love in your life to demonstrate that you are truly a child of God. Also, these three things are vital for sustaining you in times of trial, when it feels like you are in the wilderness. Each of the three has distinct characteristics uniquely their own, but they work together in the whole of your life and balance is required. If one is missing or neglected, you will lose your equilibrium and find yourself weakened and vulnerable.

The truth is that they are linked, and the bonds they have are designed by God to help us live well and happily before him, thriving for his glory. They show the glorious presence of God himself when they are tangibly demonstrated in your life. Faith, hope, and love encourage you and bear witness to those around you of the divine work taking place in your heart and life. People notice committed faith lived out, solid hope that sustains, and Christ-like love that reaches them through you.

PSALMS, HYMNS, AND SONGS

Praise God from Whom All Blessings Flow
Now Thank We All Our God
Living For Jesus

MEDITATION AND PRAYER

- What did I notice in particular about this reading?
- Did this bring to mind any recent experiences?
- Do I sense God prompting me to change or to do anything?
- I wonder . . .
- I thank God for . . .

PRAYER OF BLESSING

God of all grace, let your glory shine through tangible expressions of faith, hope, and love in the life of your servant so others may seek you, and I will be encouraged as well. In Christ, amen.

Many pieces of art and gemstones are presented with a Certificate of Authenticity. Imagine that you, as "God's workmanship" (Ephesians 2:10), are living proof to present to the world!

CERTIFICATE OF AUTHENTICITY

Since ______________________ has successfully demonstrated in action that the genuine forms of faith, hope and love are present in his/her life, it is our pleasure to present this Certificate validating that he/she is a true Christian and worthy member of the Church of Christ at ______________
Date______________
Witness #1______________________
Witness #2______________________
Witness #3______________________

Pastor ______________________

DAY 3

THE WORD OF FAITH

Romans 10:8b–9, 17 (read 5–17): "The word is near you; it is in your mouth and in your heart," that is, the message concerning faith that we proclaim: If you declare with your mouth, "Jesus is Lord," and believe in your heart that God raised him from the dead, you will be saved . . . Consequently, faith comes from hearing the message, and the message is heard through the word about Christ.

This passage is foundational to our understanding of faith, to our seeing faith as a response to God's Word and, more specifically, the Word of Christ, which is the gospel (literally the Good News). If we are to put our trust in someone or something, we need to know what we are investing our very lives in. A source of truth, or what I call *revelation,* is required. We have that in the Bible, the inspired Word of God, and in the Word made flesh: Jesus Christ who is God's living Word to us (see John 1:1 ff.).

God's Word and Christ are inseparable and work in full harmony. They offer us a unified message about God and about what he has done for us. They reveal Good News for our messy condition and direction on how to find our way through the wilderness of life.

I invite you to believe that what God says in his Word is true and completely trust in God who gave this Word and his Son to us. The Word of God is simple so we can easily understand the Good News of Jesus; yet it is complex as it goes beyond the limits of our comprehension. As you hear the Word, God by his Spirit is at work in your heart, urging you to receive his truth and say, "Yes, it is true and I believe it." Further, you must come to say from your heart, "Yes, I believe in Jesus Christ, He is my Savior and Lord." As you continue to hear and study God's Word, you can keep growing in your understanding and love for it and for Jesus.

I believe God's Word is truth, yet I know many disagree with me. We are in a time when truth is relative for many people, and so many have powerful and persuasive abilities to distort truth. The subtlety of their arguments and the skills they employ make the quest for truth even more difficult. Much of the information we get in the media—all forms and platforms—can be described as "distorted, jaundiced, counterfeit, alternative, or biased." Still, God has ways to continue communicating the Good News about Jesus Christ, who himself is the embodiment of the truth.

John's gospel in the Bible expresses beautifully the reason why his story is revealed, stating, *But these are written that you may believe that Jesus is the Christ, the Son of God, and that by believing you may have life in his name (John 20:31).*

PSALMS, HYMNS, AND SONGS

Standing on the Promises
How Firm a Foundation
Step By Step

MEDITATION AND PRAYER

- What did I notice in particular about this reading?
- Did this bring to mind any recent experiences?
- Do I sense God prompting me to change or to do anything?
- I wonder . . .
- I thank God for . . .

PRAYER OF BLESSING

Revealing God, guide me to stay close to your Word. May I keep growing in the hearing and doing of that Word, following Christ, the Word made flesh who remains with us always. Amen.

The monogram page for the Gospel of Matthew from the *Book of Kells* created in the early 8th century, illuminated richly around the Greek initials for Christ's name (Chi looks like *X*, Rho looks like *p*, Iota looks like *i*). The Scripture text in the *Book of Kells* helped preserve the written Word of God over long centuries so we can have access to Scripture today (courtesy of The Library of Trinity College, Dublin, Ireland).

TRUE FAITH DEFINED

Hebrews 11:1–2 (read 1–10): Now faith is confidence in what we hope for and assurance about what we do not see. This is what the ancients were commended for.

The author of Hebrews offers a workable definition of faith to the persecuted, dispersed, and exiled early Christians. If you read further in the eleventh chapter of the book, you will find faith showcased in the lives of many people from the Old Testament such as Abraham and Sarah. The author recognizes that faith is placed in God and lived out in both happiness and hardship.

Faith is generally seen as operating in the continuous present of our lives, a moment-by-moment trusting in God. It is closely allied with hope, which points forward to what is coming in the near term and eternally. Sometimes faith and hope are used synonymously, and in part that is what is going on in this passage.

The emphasis here is on committing to what we believe is real and true, even though it is unseen. This is belief in what God has revealed in his Word about who he eternally is and what he has done redemptively through his Son, Jesus Christ. It also develops convictions about how we ought to live in ways that honor and glorify him. In our daily walk we believe that he is present, using our faith, hope, and love to sustain us. We also discover that in the rough places, when we feel vulnerable, we are encouraged by his presence and his promises.

Faith assures us we are placed firmly in God's hand—even when we seem to have nothing to grip. We look with the eyes of faith at unseen realities surrounding us. We can also grow via information our senses provide and knowledge accumulated through study and research, but never apart from faith informed by God and his Word and our faith experiences lived out daily. All this provides us with a fuller picture of faith.

The sure conviction of these things matures us on our faith journey as we do our best to live like the faith heroes of Hebrews 11. We sometimes call this "the assurance of faith." Our assurance is strongest when we look to God and when it is based on the unseen facts we know from his Word.

If we base our assurance on our emotions and feelings alone, we are going to have a roller coaster ride. The more we look up in faith and trust, the deeper our assurance becomes. With this strong foundation, we can experience our emotions without building our faith on them. Faith helps us process what we feel and integrate those feelings with our firm foundation in God.

PSALMS, HYMNS, AND SONGS

Moment by Moment

Through It All

Psalm 121: I Lift Up My Eyes to the Mountains

MEDITATION AND PRAYER

- What did I notice in particular about this reading?
- Did this bring to mind any recent experiences?
- Do I sense God prompting me to change or to do anything?
- I wonder . . .
- I thank God for . . .

PRAYER OF BLESSING

Heavenly Father, as your servant has put true faith in you, assure me of your presence and promises. Use all your means for this, including your Word and your indwelling Holy Spirit. In Jesus's name, amen.

Faith is like a bridge that connects us to the divine. (This is Mackinac Bridge connecting the Lower and Upper Peninsulas of Michigan.)

PLACING OUR FAITH IN JESUS

John 2:11 (read 1–11): What Jesus did here in Cana of Galilee was the first of the signs through which he revealed his glory; and his disciples believed in him.

The disciples witnessed and believed in the power and glory of Jesus at the wedding in Cana. The apostle John describes it as putting their faith in him. This is one of several references to this act in the Gospel of John, and describes very clearly and simply the act of faith. It has an object: Jesus Christ. They made a commitment to him, and as the story of their lives continues throughout the New Testament we see that they lived out their commitment by following him.

It was not a light decision, for it was an action that changed their orientation and affected everything that followed for the rest of their lives. We can say that they invested everything they had in the Lord. We have already noted how faith needs knowledge about who God is and also how it requires deep trust and assurance. Here we see the commitment, the investment part of true faith.

These first disciples who put their faith in Jesus Christ did not know what it would lead to, but they were willing to follow and discover it as things unfolded. In that regard, every disciple must do the same. Faith is not just an intellectual acceptance of certain information as true. It calls us to commit to go where God leads for the rest of our lives. We go, without advance knowledge of what that going might mean.

It's amazing that those first disciples made this commitment, and it's amazing that countless people have been doing it ever since! I praise God that people whom God is drawing to himself are still making this life investment in Jesus. People from all walks of life and all over the world are doing so day after day!

The way of Jesus is open and leads us to real life today and eternal life when our purpose on earth is complete. Jesus's first disciples discovered then, and you and I discover today, what following Jesus looks like for the rest of our lives. The disciples had to grow into understanding what that meant, which took a lifetime of wrestling. They never perfected it, but they held onto their commitment and stayed the course.

And that is what we do too. There is a unique path set for each of us, with times in the wilderness during which we renew our commitment to follow Jesus. We who have placed our faith in him consciously renew that commitment daily. Keep the faith and keep going in Christ's direction!

PSALMS, HYMNS, AND SONGS

I Surrender Lord

I Have Decided To Follow Jesus

My Faith Looks Up To Thee

Psalm 31: In Thee O Lord I Put My Trust

MEDITATION AND PRAYER

- What did I notice in particular about this reading?
- Did this bring to mind any recent experiences?
- Do I sense God prompting me to change or to do anything?
- I wonder . . .
- I thank God for . . .

PRAYER OF BLESSING

Almighty and saving God, I rejoice that you receive me and all who come to you in faith. Glory be to you, author of salvation; sustain us all as we grow as disciples and experience also the demands of discipleship. In Christ, amen.

Grand Coulee Dam on the mighty Columbia River in Washington. Massive amounts of electricity are generated here, only available when tapped into. So it is with faith in God!

DAY 6

SAVED THROUGH FAITH

Romans 1:16 (read 14–17): For I am not ashamed of the gospel, because it is the power of God that brings salvation to everyone who believes: first to the Jew, then to the Gentile.

This verse is a beautiful testimony from the apostle Paul about his personal faith, as well as an eloquent witness to how important faith is in God's saving work. It is our response to the message of the gospel that God has revealed. By his direction, in ways often unrecognized, we come to hear it, embrace it as true, and put our faith in Jesus Christ. Jesus Saves!

This gracious activity is God's saving work and he expects our response. That response is what completes the picture! And what a beautiful one it is, for it is effective forever, the permanent cure to our sinful condition. It is beautiful because it is offered far and wide, to all people everywhere. The text speaks of Jew and Gentile, reflecting the division of mankind from the vantage point of the people of Israel. We might now say people of every race, color, class, language, and creed. However we like to divide up the human race cannot affect this powerful saving work of God.

The apostle Paul boldly expressed his personal embrace of the gospel, and by word and example demonstrated that he honored it, traveling as a missionary to bring the gospel to the lost. He was eager to share the Good News of his Savior and Lord. He did not intend to hide it or deny it. He was clear about what he believed and how he felt about his commitment.

We are to follow Paul's example, showing through our words and actions that we belong to Christ and desire to be known as Christians. Sometimes we may need to qualify that word *Christian* because it has so many connotations in our culture. We may need to clarify in some settings that we are *practicing* Christians, or *dedicated* Christians. Use whatever language helps indicate that you are not just going through the cultural motions but have found the gracious salvation spoken of in Romans 1:16–17. We must find ways to express what lies at the core of the Christian faith in our 21st century context.

I believe that the way we live this out reflects our faith to others. We cannot live perfect lives, nor try to pretend we can. We will be undone and called hypocrites. But we can demonstrate a genuine striving, an honest, humble presentation of who we are as Christ's disciples. Our sincere efforts to be more like Christ will give traction to our witness. This will be inviting to those we meet who are as broken and spiritually needy as we were when God's powerful work began in us. They too are in the wilderness, and we can help them find their way through it and be saved!

PSALMS, HYMNS, AND SONGS

Jesus Saves, Jesus Saves
I Will Sing Of My Redeemer
Redeemed, How I Love To Proclaim It

MEDITATION AND PRAYER

- What did I notice in particular about this reading?
- Did this bring to mind any recent experiences?
- Do I sense God prompting me to change or to do anything?
- I wonder . . .
- I thank God for . . .

PRAYER OF BLESSING

We praise and thank you, our God, that you have displayed your divine power not to destroy us but to save us. May I, your servant, know personally that power of the Gospel, and boldly share it with others. In Christ, amen.

THE POWER OF MUSTARD SEED FAITH

Matthew 17:19–20 (read 14–21): Then the disciples came to Jesus in private and asked, "Why couldn't we drive (the demon) out?" He replied, "Because you have so little faith. Truly I tell you, if you have faith as small as a mustard seed, you can say to this mountain, 'Move from here to there,' and it will move. Nothing will be impossible for you."

These words are good news for Christians who have less than a 100 percent success rate in practicing true faith. One of the people who Jesus ministered to expressed it like this: "Lord, I do believe. Help me overcome my unbelief" (Mark 9:24).

Jesus desires our complete trust in his power and grace, but we are all still working at it. My goal for this book is to help you in that process. We need to develop our faith, and I have found it is a life's work never done. But I also find that, while these words have some rebuke for my small faith, they also encourage me. Even a small amount of faith can accomplish great things, for it unites us with the unlimited power of God himself. If I discover that my faith is diminished, I can expect that, as I attend to it, my faith will grow once again.

God works through even a mustard seed-sized faith, and in his grace he will do so again and again for you and me. As Jesus often did with his first disciples, he still does for us: challenge us to deeper trust and higher expectations. We need to think far more about what can happen for those who truly believe.

May God help us trust more fully and fathom more deeply his boundless power. I love the way the apostle Paul expresses this in Ephesians 3:20–21: "Now to him who is able to do immeasurably more than all we ask or imagine, according to his power that is at work within us, to him be glory in the church and in Christ Jesus throughout all generations, for ever and ever. Amen."

God works with the little faith we bring and great things happen with his blessing. Growth happens as God uses our foundational commitments and authentic trust throughout life's journey. As our wilderness walk takes us over mountains, through deep valleys, into deserted places, or into overly crowded spaces, we experience more and more of God's power and mercy. Glory be to God!

PSALMS, HYMNS, AND SONGS

I Sing the Mighty Power of God
Only Believe
On Eagles Wings

MEDITATION AND PRAYER

- What did I notice in particular about this reading?
- Did this bring to mind any recent experiences?
- Do I sense God prompting me to change or to do anything?
- I wonder . . .
- I thank God for . . .

PRAYER OF BLESSING

God of boundless power, impress upon me, your servant, the potential that comes through faith, even a faith under development. Continue your mighty work in me every day, for your glory. In Christ alone, amen.

The General Sherman sequoia tree in Sequoia National Park, California, at 275+feet high and 36 feet wide.

The sequoia seed isn't much bigger than a penny.

THE MEASUREMENT OF GREAT FAITH

Matthew 8:8, 10 (read 5–13): The centurion replied . . . "But just say the word, and my servant will be healed." . . . When Jesus heard this, he was amazed and said to those following him, "Truly I tell you, I have not found anyone in Israel with such great faith."

While Jesus often challenged his followers by calling them people of little faith, here we have the opposite—from a Roman centurion who was clearly not (yet) a follower of Jesus. But he demonstrated himself to be truly humble before Jesus as Lord and had complete confidence in the miraculous power of Jesus. Jesus took note of this and used it as a lesson for those of us who follow him.

This is the richness of faith with which many of us struggle. We want to have complete confidence in the power of Jesus with nothing held back. Yet we struggle to surrender everything because we hope to retain some measure of control. The faith of the centurion is a beautiful story; it was this man's wonderful response that led to the lifesaving miracle that Jesus performed for his servant.

Great things come with confident faith in Jesus. Another aspect of the great faith of the centurion is his humble, selfless approach to Jesus. He was asking for Jesus's help not for himself but for a servant, not someone judged "important" or "powerful" in that culture and who would have had few options in life. There was likely nothing he stood to gain himself, other than healing for someone he valued. It is notable that this man's faith reached people outside the circle of those who thought they were God's chosen people. Christ's act embodies love and brings glory to God the Father for all to witness.

I believe there is a lesson here about developing confidence in our faith not only for our needs but for the needs of others. As we look outside our personal spaces we can easily discover people and ministries that are struggling in the wilderness experiences of life. Great faith stretches us to look to Christ for those who are laid upon our hearts, expecting that he will bring aid.

Faith can help us past the helpless feeling that can occur in the face of great need. We can intercede for those far off, assist those who are near, and confidently approach Christ asking for his demonstration of mercy for all.

PSALMS, HYMNS, AND SONGS

All Earth to Him, Her Homage Brings
People Need the Lord
If You But Trust in God to Guide You
Learning To Lean On Jesus

MEDITATION AND PRAYER

- What did I notice in particular about this reading?
- Did this bring to mind any recent experiences?
- Do I sense God prompting me to change or to do anything?
- I wonder . . .
- I thank God for . . .

PRAYER OF BLESSING

O Lord, move your humble servant to a greater faith, and enable me to experience that growth within my heart and in loving service to others, in Christ's name and after his example, amen.

Needing trust in a higher helping hand!

FAITH AND DOUBT IN THE STORMS

Matthew 14:25b–31 (read 22–34): Jesus went out to them, walking on the lake. When the disciples saw him . . . they were terrified . . . "Take courage! It is I. Don't be afraid." "Lord, if it's you," Peter replied, "tell me to come to you on the water." "Come," he said. Then Peter got down out of the boat, walked on the water and came toward Jesus. But when he saw the wind, he was afraid and, beginning to sink, cried out, "Lord, save me!" Immediately Jesus reached out his hand and caught him. "You of little faith," he said, "why did you doubt?"

I am struck by the boldness of Peter in this dramatic appearance by Jesus. Peter seems to be testing Jesus with his request, "if it's you tell me to come to you on the water." Knowing Peter, maybe there was some impetuous bravado mixed in with his faith. If so, it would seem Peter failed the test when he began to sink. Was it his self-confidence that led to his failure? I think so. Surely his faith in Jesus wavered, and Jesus reprimanded him for his lack of faith.

Complete reliance on Christ working through him would have led to a different outcome. Peter instead fixed his focus on the waves and the storm's threat, which led to failure. Christ came to the disciples on the water to reveal his power and glory so they would grow their trust in him. They had a lot to learn about this, and this would not be Peter's last lesson.

Neither has your or my last faith lesson occurred. Jesus caught Peter with his hand, and our Lord continues to reach out to each of us when we get that sinking feeling. His grace continues to reach us even as his deepest desire is that we grow in faith and into complete reliance on him.

Keeping your focus fixed on Christ is the abiding lesson here. He has power over all things and wants to help you. When you are in challenging situations, one of the temptations is to just go it alone. "I can handle this all by myself," you say to yourself. That's when you may discover the truth of the old proverb, "Pride goes before the fall."

By relying on him, you can step out in faith and do incredible things. Your faith connects you to the grace and power of our Lord. The apostle

Paul stated it like this: *"I can do everything through him who gives me strength"* Phil. 4:13. He spoke about life's adversities as well as its blessings, coping with it all by faith in Jesus "in plenty and in want." Keep your eyes on Jesus in every circumstance!

PSALMS, HYMNS, AND SONGS

Through It All
Psalm 73, In Doubt and Temptation
Turn Your Eyes Upon Jesus
In The Hour of Trial

MEDITATION AND PRAYER

- What did I notice in particular about this reading?
- Does this bring to mind any recent experiences?
- Do I sense God prompting me to change or to do anything?
- I wonder . . .
- I thank God for . . .

PRAYER OF BLESSING

O God who gives endurance and encouragement, be close to me in the times of trial. Guide me to rely ever more fully upon you and help me face any fears and doubts that arise. In Christ's strong name, amen.

Surfing may not be walking on water, but it still takes courage!

FAITH AND PRAYER

Matthew 21:21–22 (read 18–22): Jesus replied, "Truly I tell you, if you have faith and do not doubt, not only can you do what was done to the fig tree, but also you can say to this mountain, 'Go, throw yourself into the sea,' and it will be done. If you believe, you will receive whatever you ask for in prayer."

This is a striking text! It describes mountain-moving faith and challenges us to think really big. As we measure the personal obstacles before us, such faith opens up huge possibilities. Our God is the God of possibilities, who long before challenged Abraham by asking, *"Is anything too hard for the Lord?" (Gen. 18:14)*

He is Almighty and we are not, yet Jesus teaches us that faith unadulterated by doubt can lead to great things happening, things we could call miraculous and unprecedented. I love the perspective this brings that draws us out of our often-limited faith. Our minds can put walls around the arenas where we think God operates. This limited thinking shows up in our prayers. Ponder what you ask for as well as the requests you don't express, and ask yourself what this says about your view of God. J. B. Phillips wrote a book some years ago titled, *How Big is Your God?* I ask you, how big is your God today?

This passage in Matthew urges us to think big and pray boldly—for our daily needs, but also for things that seem immovable, changeless, and crushing. Dare we add *hopeless* to this list? As we strive to pray with a doubt-free faith, we need to grow in our knowledge and trust of the God revealed in the Bible. This happens by studying the Bible and time in prayer.

There is a limitless horizon before us when we pray in faith, as huge and wide as the western prairies of the United States. As we look up to the clear night sky, we see no limits there; we see innumerable stars, the same stars promised by God to represent the children of Abraham and Sarah!

I also pray for God's wisdom in what I seek. I don't want magical performances to deepen my faith. I want to request things that will demonstrate the glory of God and the witness of Jesus in my life. Jesus doesn't put limits on what I can ask for in prayer, though I confess that I limit myself. I feel like there are appropriate things to ask for and others that are foolish and will be unanswered. God puts no limits on prayer.

I invite you to wrestle, to challenge yourselves to affirm how great your God is, to take down the constraints your mind or your tradition has placed on Almighty God. *Believe and receive.*

PSALMS, HYMNS, AND SONGS

Psalm 40: I Waited For the Lord Most High
If You and I Believe In Christ
How Great Thou Art

MEDITATION AND PRAYER

- What did I notice in particular about this reading?
- Did this bring to mind any recent experiences?
- Do I sense God prompting me to change or to do anything?
- I wonder . . .
- I thank God for . . .

PRAYER OF BLESSING

Everlasting God, Creator of the universe, enable your servant's vision to grow, hear the prayers that I offer. Give me wisdom to pray along with your will, insofar as I can discern it. In Jesus's name, amen.

Denali, rising through the clouds at 20,310 feet, at the Denali National Park and Preserve in Alaska.

THE EFFECTS OF FAITH FRIENDS

Luke 5:18–20, 24b–25 (read 17–26): Some men came carrying a paralyzed man on a mat and tried to take him into the house to lay him before Jesus. When they could not find a way to do this because of the crowd, they went up on the roof and lowered him on his mat through the tiles into the middle of the crowd, right in front of Jesus. When Jesus saw their faith, he said, "Friend, your sins are forgiven . . . I tell you, get up, take your mat and go home." Immediately he stood up in front of them, took what he had been lying on and went home praising God.

The paralytic and his friends had faith in Jesus and not a passive faith where they just "let it happen." They took active measures to get the man to Jesus for healing, and Jesus responded. He restored the man to health, and graciously included a fuller restoration in his pardon for sin. This led to controversy with the Pharisees nearby, whom he rebuked and then used the occasion to show his divine authority.

I want to focus on how faith operated here in a communal way. Jesus embraced the restored man and his friends, and the Gospel of Luke tells us he acted when he saw *their* faith. This word is important to notice because it tells us an important truth about the effects that can occur when believing people work together. Working together may be praying for someone in need; it could apply to people united in heart and purpose for a particular endeavor; and it would readily include people of faith sincerely praying for their church or another church undergoing persecution.

While I talk of faith being expressed in prayer, we see from this account in Luke that faith is also expressed in action. The friends moved and acted boldly in their faith. When people of faith seek God's help together, they move toward the solution.

This principle is instructive and challenges us individually and corporately to ask, "What am I doing with my faith concern? How can I be part of the solution?" We seek divine help, but also discover that we are part of the solution as God works through us. He can work apart from us, of course, but he has chosen through the ages to also work through groups of faithful people, whether two or three, or hundreds, or even thousands. When we are united together in common purpose, he receives the glory.

PSALMS, HYMNS, AND SONGS

Psalm 133: How Good and Pleasant Is the Sight

Blest Be the Tie That Binds

The Servant Song

MEDITATION AND PRAYER

- What did I notice in particular about this reading?
- Did this bring to mind any recent experiences?
- Do I sense God prompting me to change or to do anything?
- I wonder . . .
- I thank God for . . .

PRAYER OF BLESSING

God of your people, thank you for Christian community. Bless me with supportive friends, and open my eyes to opportunities to act in faith to assist others. In the name and after the model of Jesus, amen.

Circle of Friends

FAITH PRESERVED THROUGH TRIAL

Luke 22:31–32 (read 24–34): "Simon, Simon, Satan has asked to sift all of you as wheat. But I have prayed for you, Simon, that your faith may not fail. And when you have turned back, strengthen your brothers."

Jesus spoke these words to Peter during the Last Supper, with Jesus's betrayal imminent and his death on the Roman cross soon to follow. Peter's denial was foreseen by our Lord, yet Jesus's gracious love comes through in these comforting words. Jesus knows the temptation and failure that will come, but he will not let Peter go.

This is a powerful declaration of the role of our Savior as our Intercessor. He demonstrates one of his priestly functions by interceding for Peter during his testing. We must remember this when we face trials during life's wilderness times. We can also find comfort in this intercession when we are burdened by the trials people we love are going through and are fervently praying for them.

Let us not forget that we have a Savior who reigns at the right hand of the Father in glory! He is praying for us and conveying our struggling words, clarifying them as the best editor we will ever have. I pray that as you read these words it reminds you of this dimension of Christ's work for you. Your faith in Jesus assures that he is praying for you as he did for Peter.

While this text reveals Christ as intercessor, it also shows his gracious work in enabling us to keep the faith. We are not passive in this endeavor, but need to persevere in faith and attend to its development. We are to hold firmly to our trust in the Lord, but his grip is stronger on us than ours on him. That knowledge increases my level of assurance and, I pray, yours as well. We will not be abandoned in our trials, but in them can cling to Christ and know he is going through them with us.

The text also speaks of the blessings that flow through us when we are sustained in trial and restored in grace. Peter later would become a source of strength to the other disciples as he took leadership during hard times. God can do the same through you and me as he uses our experiences to make our faith stronger and as we develop more understanding and credibility. We can be especially helpful to fellow travelers on the faith journey who are going through things we have already experienced. Praise God he does not discard us. He recycles us and improves us for ongoing service in his kingdom!

PSALMS, HYMNS, AND SONGS

Psalm 66: O All You People Bless Our God
I Know Whom I Have Believed
In The Hour of Trial
How Firm a Foundation

MEDITATION AND PRAYER

- What did I notice in particular about this reading?
- Did this bring to mind any recent experiences?
- Do I sense God prompting me to change or to do anything?
- I wonder . . .
- I thank God for . . .

PRAYER OF BLESSING

Gracious Father, hear the intercessions of your beloved Son on my behalf, and fortify me with the knowledge that I have the Savior advocating for me. Use me also to bless others. For Christ's sake, amen.

My Kansas friends harvest wheat so much faster than the sifting methods of old.

FAITH LIKE ABRAHAM, FATHER OF BELIEVERS

Romans 4:1–3 (read 1–12): What then shall we say that Abraham, our forefather according to the flesh, discovered in this matter? If, in fact, Abraham was justified by works, he had something to boast about—but not before God. What does the Scripture say? "Abraham believed God, and it was credited to him as righteousness."

Abraham and Sarah lived by faith, responding to God's call to leave Ur and move to where he would direct them to go. They knew about uncharted life in the wilderness like few others, but still trusted and obeyed God. The book of Genesis records the many trials and challenges that developed the couple's faith over a long lifetime. Abraham has descendants by genetic lineage and also by belief in Christ as Father of believers. In Romans 4:16 it states that all believers are *"of the faith of Abraham. He is the father of us all."*

Our text focuses on the effect of faith, which led to Abraham being credited with righteousness before God even though he was far from perfect. In the light of the New Testament (including several chapters in the letter to the Romans), we have come to understand this concept as *justification.*

Briefly stated, the concept is that the righteousness of Christ becomes ours when we believe and are saved. His perfect righteousness blankets over our sin so our sinful record is covered; the judgment that should rightly fall upon us was taken to the cross by Christ on our behalf. We would never be able to accomplish this by ourselves or through our best works. Our only effective response is faith, and the results are amazing and eternal. Cherish this work accomplished by Christ on our behalf.

The response of faith provides us with a lifetime of Christ's righteousness, which we claim now as our own. And it must propel us to live up to that declaration so we live as those redeemed by Christ and clothed in his righteousness. Our lives need to reflect his perfect, humble love and obedience. Our desire should be to become more like him before the face of God—and also in the observations of those who know us.

Let that be your daily endeavor! It is perhaps best stated like this: "Become what you are!"

PSALMS, HYMNS, AND SONGS

We Are Pilgrims on a Journey
When Peace Like a River
Not What My Hands Have Done

MEDITATION AND PRAYER

- What did I notice in particular about this reading?
- Did this bring to mind any recent experiences?
- Do I sense God prompting me to change or to do anything?
- I wonder . . .
- I thank God for . . .

PRAYER OF BLESSING

God of Abraham and Sarah, let me joyfully wear the clothing of righteousness received from Christ as I continue on the long pilgrimage of faith. For Jesus's sake, amen.

Rembrandt's etching "Abraham and Isaac" (1645) that depicts the test of Abraham's faith at Mt. Moriah recorded in Genesis 22.

LIVING BY FAITH IN THE PRESENT

Galatians 2:20 (read 17–21): I have been crucified with Christ and I no longer live, but Christ lives in me. The life I now live in the body, I live by faith in the Son of God, who loved me and gave himself for me.

From an early age we ask the question, "Who am I?" We try to discern who we are while also differentiating ourselves from others. We know we exist and we have a unique identity all our own. We continue to grow in our sense of personhood, but when we put our faith in Christ another dimension to our identity blossoms. We do not become another person, yet we sense the indwelling presence of Christ and, with careful attention, begin to notice change.

As this change occurs over time, we discern Christ's control in our thoughts, desires, values, and character. He is remodeling our inner self as we trust in him. The process goes faster when we allow him to refashion us to be like him instead of fighting every step of the way. What has been corrupted by sin dies off, and what honors Christ flourishes. Depending on your spiritual condition when you put your faith in him, you may have seen dramatic changes or you may sense smaller, incremental changes.

The process of personal reformation will continue all your life as you live by faith in the Son of God. Your gratitude will grow as you treasure what it means that he loved you and gave himself for you.

This goes to a much deeper level than simply affirming that "Jesus died for the sins of the world." It embeds into your inner life, the heart out of which the issues of life flow. It brings you to say in wonder, "Jesus died for me, yes *me*, and he loves me!" It affirms to you that Christ lives within you. If you look in a mirror or someone takes a picture of you, the image is you, of course. But the "real you" of your innermost self is fully affected by Christ.

There is a parallel in what happens when two people have a deep and committed love for one another. There is something hard to describe about that connection, but the bond of love is strong and part of each person. Also with Christ, where there are dimensions that lie beyond description, it's sometimes described in mystical terms and sometimes in terms of deep inner feelings.

Our characters are each unique, with the Spirit of God moving in diverse ways within us and the faith communities that shape us. Now it becomes an invitation for you to experience this by faith in your life day by day! How can you describe such wonder?

PSALMS, HYMNS, AND SONGS

Living for Jesus
Now I Belong To Jesus
I am His and He is Mine
And Can It Be
Come to us, Beloved Stranger

MEDITATION AND PRAYER

- What did I notice in particular about this reading?
- Did this bring to mind any recent experiences?
- Do I sense God prompting me to change or to do anything?
- I wonder . . .
- I thank God for . . .

PRAYER OF BLESSING

Creating and Redeeming God, help me grow in Christian identity and assist me to integrate all of life into the eternal life of our blessed Savior and Lord, in whose name we pray. Amen.

What is your real identity?

GETTING A HANDLE ON HOPE

Romans 8:24–25 (read 18–25): For in this hope we were saved. But hope that is seen is no hope at all. Who hopes for what they already have? But if we hope for what we do not yet have, we wait for it patiently.

Hope is used in a number of grammatical ways including as a noun, which stands for a reality possessed. Using it as a noun I can say, "I have hope . . . My hope comes from God." It can also be used as a verb, which signifies an action. I can say in the wilderness, "I hope for a way through this."

One way I like to understand this is that hope is a gift from God that he graciously gives to all who are saved (a noun). But it is also our response (a verb), our action of trusting for the future. As we trust in Christ each moment and as we project that forward into the immediate and eternal future, hope has Spandex®-like qualities that stretch endlessly throughout our lives.

Hope is unseen, with the text making it clear that hope's very nature embraces the unseen. We can't hold it, we cannot package it, we cannot eat or drink it. But that doesn't make it unreal. We are not talking here of a mere wish or imagined future. We are reflecting on a possession that sustains us over our life's journey and is fulfilled when one day we shall be eternally in God's presence.

That destination is described in Hebrews 11:10 as, "the city with foundations, whose architect and builder is God." I believe wholly that this is not some illusory castle in the sky, but a place where I shall be with God as an eternal part of his kingdom. My prayer is that you also have this hope. Hope keeps us going with its amazing power to sustain us and encourage us forward.

The text speaks about waiting for hope patiently, one taste of the rich biblical teaching focused on waiting upon the Lord (cf. Isaiah 40:31). The language in the original Greek speaks of a sense of enduring, of holding up. Patience can be misunderstood as forced inaction or repression of activity. That is the opposite of what the Word tells us about hope.

We wait for hope by depending on it, standing tall upon it as the foundation that sustains us, affirming that ultimately that foundation is none other than the Living God. Stand firm in hope!

PSALMS, HYMNS, AND SONGS

Come Thou Long Expected Jesus
My Hope Is Built On Nothing Less
On Jordan's Stormy Bank

MEDITATION AND PRAYER

- What did I notice in particular about this reading?
- Did this bring to mind any recent experiences?
- Do I sense God prompting me to change or do anything?
- I wonder . . .
- I thank God for . . .

PRAYER OF BLESSING

Holy God, we cannot behold you directly now, but we do have hope in the unseen and eternal. Assist me to be well grounded in hope and discover daily the strength you impart, until I can behold you in your glory. For Christ's sake, amen.

Unseen beauty is revealed in a coconut agate from Mexico and an Oregon Thunderegg Agate, which I cut and polished.

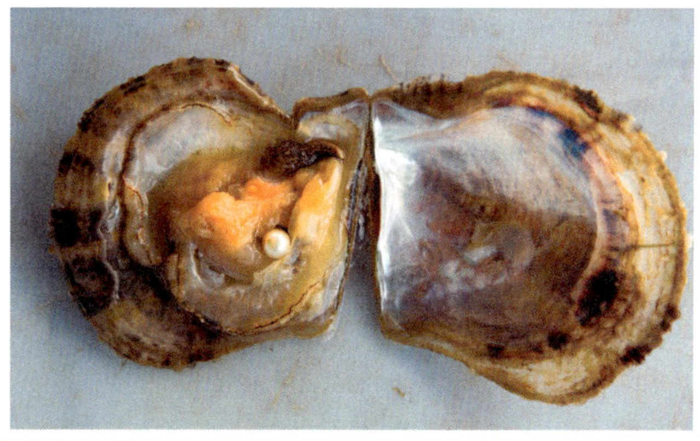

A beautiful pearl hidden in an oyster!

THE SOURCE OF OVERFLOWING HOPE

Romans 15:13 (read 7–13): May the God of hope fill you with all joy and peace as you trust in him, so that you may overflow with hope by the power of the Holy Spirit.

This verse takes the form of a benediction—a blessing expressed—and highlights that our God is the God of hope. He is the source of hope in the fullness of his Triune Majesty. Christ came to earth to bring hope to a lost world. Particular emphasis is given here to the powerful work of the Holy Spirit to generate hope in us—at such levels that it spills over to share with others. Wow! I need this God of hope in my life, and I often reread this verse as blessing and inspiration. I invite you to regularly do the same.

Life's challenging experiences can take a lot of hope energy from our personal reserves, and in really rough stretches it may seem that we are close to being hopeless. As a trusting child of God, we are never truly hopeless. But the perception is that our spiritual hope tank is just about on E—Empty. We need to keep an eye on our hope tank to avoid despair.

Thankfully, the divine source is always available for us to come close to him for regular fill-ups. Don't contaminate this energy source with substitutes or knock-offs like illusionary escape, self-help band-aids, or easy solutions from religious charlatans. Only that which is from God will do, the God known through faith in Jesus Christ and channeled to us through the Spirit's work. Also, don't let pride enter the picture. It is God's hope that holds you up in times of trial, not your own strength.

This hope will enable you to keep going forward no matter what. It will work through you to encourage those close to you to persevere and go the distance. It will spill out from you to the truly hopeless—those who are desperate, whose future appears hopeless, and who populate your neighborhood, your city, and the world.

May your words, attitudes, love, and servant heart demonstrate to all that Christ is in you, the hope of glory. As the Father in heaven gives you his benediction and hope fills you, pass it along. Tell others what your source is; point them to the Way in Jesus so they too may join in glorifying the Father, Son, and Holy Spirit. Unto God alone be all glory.

PSALMS, HYMNS, AND SONGS

Lord of All Hopefulness
For The Gift of God the Spirit
Breathe On Me Breath of God
There Is A Redeemer

MEDITATION AND PRAYER

- What did I notice in particular about this reading?
- Did this bring to mind any recent experiences?
- Do I sense God prompting me to change or to do anything?
- I wonder . . .
- I thank God for . . .

PRAYER OF BLESSING

God of hope, work in me daily by your Holy Spirit so that hope grows in me, encourages me, and overflows into the lives of others. Glory be to you, source of hope, in Christ our Savior's name, amen.

Niagara Falls located at Niagara Falls, New York, and in Ontario, Canada.

DAY 17

PUTTING YOUR HOPE IN JESUS

1 Timothy 4:9–10 (read 9–11, 17–19): This is a trustworthy saying that deserves full acceptance. That is why we labor and strive, because we have put our hope in the living God, who is the Savior of all people, and especially of those who believe.

We looked at the act of putting our faith in Jesus in an earlier chapter. The action described here—putting our hope in God—is integrally connected with faith. Both are actions of commitment to the Lord, seen from different angles. I think of faith as active in each moment, and as faith stretches into the future it becomes hope in God. Faith is "now;" hope is "then." Faith and hope are like fraternal twins: close, but distinguishable. We are saved by grace through putting our faith in Christ; we are sustained in grace as we put our hope in Christ for the rest of our lives. Faith is conviction; hope is reason for perseverance.

This challenge to "put our hope in the living God" points to the complete investment of our lives in him as the Triune God. Financial advisors tell us to diversify our investments. Our culture advises us to diversify the investment of our lives in many places, increasingly urging us to be religiously inclusive as well. The Word of God urges us to commit what we are and will be to God alone.

Hope enables us to realize that life will always and only be sustained in the living God. The bleak alternative is hopelessness and death. This is the core of the gospel, a truth in which the apostle Paul had invested his labor and strength. He uses it here as a motto for Christians to hear through the generations. It is his testimony and a testimony for other believers to repeat to those they can influence. You can create your own version of "I have put my hope in the Living God, my Savior."

Look within your heart and review the evidence of your life—have you put your hope in the living God? Does this hope affect your desires and aspirations, affect all your life goals? Do you have the peace that comes to those who have this sure hope of salvation?

My prayer is that you do, and experience life abundantly and richly with him as your loving and gracious Lord. This fits well with Jesus's desire that we seek first his kingdom in our heart, home, and all areas of life. One day, the full and perfect experience of this hope will be ours to cherish forever.

PSALMS, HYMNS, AND SONGS

My Life is in You Lord
My Hope is Built on Nothing Less
My Hope is in the Lord
Psalm 16, When In the Night I Meditate

MEDITATION AND PRAYER

- What did I notice in particular about this reading?
- Did this bring to mind any recent experiences?
- Do I sense God prompting me to change or do anything?
- I wonder . . .
- I thank God for . . .

PRAYER OF BLESSING

God of hope, continue blessing your servant and help me in the ongoing affirmation of commitment to you in all seasons of life. Encourage all of your servants in the possession of the only hope that lasts. In Christ, amen.

An illuminated illustration of Elizabeth and the Virgin Mary, The Visitation, within a Book of Hours, a medieval devotional (M 96, Folio 50, The Walters Art Gallery, Baltimore, MD).

I like to think of it as Elizabeth placing a hand on hope!

PROJECTING A HOPEFUL FUTURE

2 Corinthians 1:8b, 10–11a (read 3–11): We despaired of life itself . . . He has delivered us from such a deadly peril, and he will deliver us again. On him we have set our hope that he will continue to deliver us, as you help us by your prayers.

The early church faced intense persecution, as some believers still do today in tragic ways. In this text, Paul describes the effect persecution had on him. It is instructive for all who face trials to know that deep despair can occur, that we totter on the edge of the abyss of utter hopelessness. Paul was delivered many times throughout his ministry through very dark times, and the same God who delivered Paul will now carry you.

Hope does not die, but instead thrives once again because God remains with us. Even when we come to the end of our lives, we are delivered from death to eternal life. The ultimate goal of our hope is met when we join God in his eternal home forever.

The apostle Paul was delivered by God out of a deep personal trial and was able to again set his hope on him. The words Paul expresses here convey his experiences so others can be encouraged to set their hope in the Lord during tough times. God delivered, with the emphasis falling on the ongoing dimension of this in that "he will continue to deliver us." Hope brings confidence for the future, knowing that hope will never run out as we keep following God's way.

One more important thing to notice is how the hope we place in God is assisted by the intercessory prayer of others. Paul was conscious of this and wanted the church in Corinth to know how vital it was. When you are in the wilderness, you need to share your struggle with others to gain prayer support. When you silently suffer, you cut yourself off from resources God provides. Don't let pride close down channels of grace when you desperately need them. Communicate your concerns and ask for prayer!

Likewise, you need to be an intercessor when you become aware of others' burdens or concerns. They need your support. Pray sincerely, trusting that God works along with the prayers of his people. Let others know you are lifting them up in prayer. The knowledge that others are praying sustains those who are down. It is one way that God uses to nurture hope in his children as they continue the often arduous march to the City of God.

PSALMS, HYMNS, AND SONGS

His Eye Is On the Sparrow
He Leadeth Me
O Love That Will Not Let Me Go
Day by Day

MEDITATION AND PRAYER

- What did I notice in particular about this reading?
- Did this bring to mind any recent experiences?
- Did I sense God prompting me to change or to do anything?
- I wonder . . .
- I thank God for . . .

PRAYER OF BLESSING

Father of mercies and God of all compassion, hold fast to your servant in times of trial and temptation. Guide me through all the perils of life and bring me into your eternal home, prepared by Jesus in whom we pray, amen.

Song Sparrow
"Are not two sparrows sold for a penny? Yet not one of them will fall to the ground outside your Father's care" (Matthew 10:29). Look up the promise given in 1 Corinthians 10:13 in your Bible.

THE CONSTRUCTION OF HOPE

Romans 5:1–5: Therefore, since we have been justified through faith, we have peace with God through our Lord Jesus Christ, through whom we have gained access by faith into this grace in which we now stand. And we boast in the hope of the glory of God. Not only so, but we also glory in our sufferings, because we know that suffering produces perseverance; perseverance, character; and character, hope. And hope does not put us to shame, because God's love has been poured out into our hearts through the Holy Spirit, who has been given to us.

Do you rejoice always? I can only say I am working on it. The conclusion of these verses today points out how we are enabled to rejoice. God's love fills our hearts, and the Holy Spirit is at work to develop our rich response to that love, which also embraces hope. Our hope is to be "in the glory of God." Let's look at this on two levels.

First is that when God is present, his glory is manifested. He has promised to never leave or forsake us, so his glory is present with us each day and shines forth even when the surroundings seem dark. When the clouds are lifted we may sense God's presence more easily, though hope affirms He is present all the time. We don't have a pillar and a cloud to see as the Israelites did in the wilderness; instead, we have faith in the unseen and use the "eyes of our hearts" (Eph. 1:18) to know the hope to which we are called.

The second level is this: putting our hope in God points us toward the ultimate fulfillment when we are raised from the dead. We shall fully and eternally be in the glorious presence of God and reigning with Christ in his kingdom.

Hope is a building project in our lives. I like projects and usually have several unfinished projects going on. But not all projects are fun. Some run into obstacles, and with some it seems several of Murphy's Laws are fulfilled. I wrestle with becoming angry and having a jaded attitude. As projects continue toward completion, often a new day brings fresh ideas to solve the problem and I get closer to completion. I continue and rejoice when I have reached the goal.

In the building project God has undertaken to perfect Christ in each of us, *"the Hope of Glory,"* we will go through hard times. Plus, God has flawed materials to work with. Suffering in many forms may be our experience, and perseverance is necessary as we wrestle with circumstances. Character develops as we are tempered in the trials of life. But these trials also develop hope! Hope grows through it all, and the result is becoming complete in the presence of God forever.

PSALMS, HYMNS, AND SONGS

God Leads His Dear Children Along
All The Way My Savior Leads Me
He Leadeth Me
He Giveth More Grace

MEDITATION AND PRAYER

- What did I notice in particular about this reading?
- Did this bring to mind any recent experiences?
- Do I sense God prompting me to change or to do anything?
- I wonder . . .
- I thank God for . . .

PRAYER OF BLESSING

O God our Maker, continue your work of sanctification and in the construction of hope in my life. Uphold me in the challenges that occur and assist me to persevere, empowered by the Holy Spirit, in the name and strength of the Lord Jesus, amen.

Meijer Gardens and Sculpture Park in Grand Rapids, Michigan, one of our favorite local places, undergoing another huge addition (courtesy of Owens Ames Kimball).

DAY 20

HOPE AGAINST HOPE

Romans 4:16b–18 (read 13–25): [Abraham] is the father of us all. As it is written: "I have made you a father of many nations." He is our father in the sight of God, in whom he believed—the God who gives life to the dead and calls into being things that were not. Against all hope, Abraham in hope believed and so became the father of many nations, just as it had been said to him, "So shall your offspring be."

Hope in God and his Word operates in the unseen. Hope enables us to be shaped into the perfect vessel to receive what God has promised us he will supply. When we receive God's gifts, we can state with certainty that our hope has been fulfilled. Our confidence was always grounded in God; it was never a dream or fantasy.

Unbelievers may ridicule us; our own supporters may lose heart. Sometimes shaping the vessel (us!) takes quite a long time—more time than we would plan if we controlled things. God always provides at the right time from his divine perspective.

Abraham and Sarah waited a long time for the son God promised them; the Israelites waited generations for the Root of Jesse, the Son of David (Jesus) to arrive. You may be waiting a long time for God's answers and help; and we wait for the return of Jesus, the Son of God. All of these things are represented in what this portion of Scripture says about Abraham. For *"against all hope, Abraham in hope believed"* (in God's promises), and so shall we!

We once drove through Death Valley in California. It was hot, dry, and desolate, but at the same time it was strikingly beautiful to see the depths of the valley against the foothills rising above it. Color was everywhere in sand and stone, shifting with the sun and shadow over multiple textures and heights. We could see lilac tints in the distance. It was foreboding but impressive. I hope someday to travel there when a super bloom is underway because then this barren place rivals the best gardens in the world.

Life abounds in Death Valley despite the heat and arid conditions, hidden until conditions are perfect for life to blossom. At the right time, for those of us who hope in God, the glorious presence of our Maker shines forth.

God fulfills our hopes in his time. The true conclusion will be when the Trumpet of God sounds, we are changed, and we enter into our eternal home prepared by Jesus in his glorious Kingdom.

PSALMS, HYMNS, AND SONGS

Psalm 40: I Waited For the Lord Most High

If You But Trust in God to Guide You

Lo How A Rose E'er Blooming

The King Shall Come When the Morning Dawns

Come Ye Faithful Raise the Strain

MEDITATION AND PRAYER

- What did I notice in particular about this reading?
- Did this bring to mind any recent experiences?
- Do I sense God prompting me to change or to do anything?
- I wonder . . .
- I thank God for . . .

PRAYER OF BLESSING

Eternal God, God of Abraham and Sarah, and God of me, your child, when roadblocks and obstacles seem insurmountable, remind me of Abraham, who believed in hope. In Jesus's name, amen.

Death Valley National Park in California

A GOOD HOPE

2 Thessalonians 2:16–17 (read 13–17): May our Lord Jesus Christ himself and God our Father, who loved us and by his grace gave us eternal encouragement and good hope, encourage your hearts and strengthen you in every good deed and word.

Hope is coupled with eternal encouragement, both coming as gifts of God's grace. I see the two integrating nicely together, trusting they are at work in your life! What I want you to notice is the adjective given for hope, namely "good." Something inside of me wants to say, shouldn't that be "best" or "greatest?" I could think this is too plain. I could struggle in describing it in terms of the endearing ways little children use comparative language when they are early in their language skills, perhaps calling hope "the gooderest" or "the most besterest!" What I understand better through my study of the original language is that what we translate here as "good" really has a utilitarian aspect to it. It is good in terms of being rightly fitted for the task it was designed for. Perhaps cooks turn to their "good pan," mechanics to their "good wrench." That's the one they prefer for it is best designed for their task, in their experience.

So with "good hope," what is revealed is richer than saying "what a nice hope." It tells us we have the right hope, the very best that could be designed because our Maker fashioned it for us. This is the one that will get the job done. My friends, you have that kind of hope. It's not some cheap knockoff that will fail you. I once had a supposed Crescent wrench look-a-like that was useless, before I bought a real one and discarded the other. The hope God gives will Is be reliable, so you can keep using it every day. It will not fail you.

Make sure your hope is the good one in this sense, and that you haven't been duped by some imposter. Some people are deluded in thinking hope lies in themselves, their assets, or their social networks. There are other alleged versions of what hope is but be assured that this one, revealed by God, is the real thing. As the text states, it comes from God himself. It is part of the wonderful package of grace that he freely gives you in his beloved Son. Use it, enjoy it!

PSALMS, HYMNS, AND SONGS

My Hope Is Built On Nothing Less
In Christ Alone, My Hope Is Found
Blessed Assurance, Jesus Is Mine
If You But Trust in God to Guide You

MEDITATION AND PRAYER

- What did I notice in particular about this reading?
- Did this bring to mind any recent experiences?
- Do I sense God prompting me to change or to do anything?
- I wonder . . .
- I thank God for . . .

PRAYER OF BLESSING

God of truth, enable me to discern the good hope that you provide because so many counterfeits are offered in our culture. May I know that your hope is suitable for each trial in my life, along with your eternal encouragement. For Christ's sake, amen.

This is a picture of my "good hammer." Fifty years ago I asked my Dad, Gerrit Molenbeek, a cabinetmaker, what brand would be a good hammer. He suggested a Stanley, so I bought one. While I now have others, this is still my "good one."

HOPE AS AN ANCHOR

Hebrews 6:19–20 (read 13–20): We have this hope as an anchor for the soul, firm and secure. It enters the inner sanctuary behind the curtain, where our forerunner Jesus, has entered on our behalf. He has become a high priest forever, in the order of Melchizedek.

As the early Christians were dispersed by persecution, they traveled by land and sea to various places seeking safety. We've talked about our desire for a firm and secure foundation of faith as we travel the wilderness of life. As we think this time about sea travel, we envision calm waters and a safe harbor to shelter us from life's storms. This verse offers us the image of hope as an anchor for our souls.

Like God himself and the hope we have in him, all is unseen. The anchor should be secured at the seafloor with a rope attaching it to the ship from below. As the author of Hebrews develops this metaphor, he tells us that the anchor is safe not beneath us but actually above us. By faith we are moored to the Holy Place in heaven where God dwells.

Using Old Testament imagery, which is common in this letter, he speaks of a heavenly representation of the Holy of Holies, located in the inner sanctuary of the temple. Jesus has taken the anchor to its heavenly counterpart where God is and where it is eternally secured. That work is part of his priestly role as our Intercessor. He understands our plight and is looking out for us as our Savior.

If the ship of your life is rolling about and winds are gusting, remember that there is an unseen anchor holding you fast. You may rock and roll (!) but he will keep you from a shipwreck. As you trust in him, grip the rope firmly as it disappears into the water and know that It is tied to the anchor—secured with God.

Jesus was often near or on the Sea of Galilee during his public ministry and demonstrated to the disciples his power over the forces of nature there. He told them, "Don't be afraid." May Jesus say the same to you when anxieties occur. When we look to the Savior, we find peace. His presence remains with us in every trial here on earth, while he is also interceding for us at the right hand of God, the Father Almighty. What a Savior, what a Friend we have in Jesus!

PSALMS, HYMNS, AND SONGS

In Times like These
The Solid Rock
How Sweet the Name of Jesus Sounds
In the Hour of Trial

MEDITATION AND PRAYER

- What did I notice in particular about this reading?
- Did this bring to mind any recent experiences?
- Do I sense God prompting me to change or to do anything?
- I wonder . . .
- I thank God for . . .

PRAYER OF BLESSING

Almighty God, build assurance in me day by day, that I am securely anchored in the heavenly haven where you dwell eternally, where Jesus has gone ahead of us preparing a place. In his name, amen.

THE DEFENSE OF HOPE

1 Peter 3:15–16 (read 13–18a): But in your hearts revere Christ as Lord. Always be prepared to give an answer to everyone who asks you to give the reason for the hope that you have. But do this with gentleness and respect, keeping a clear conscience, so that those who speak maliciously against your good behavior in Christ may be ashamed of their slander.

We are told in this verse about the importance of having a defense for the hope that is in us. That can be for both the possession of hope as a gift from God, and the active hope we develop in our hearts and lives. In a broader view, it could be for the entire truth of the gospel of Christ, who is our hope. We do not need to develop an elaborate defense of this—that would be epistle length, although it can be done, and Christian scholars write about this in the field called Apologetics.

More practically, it is an invitation to tell those we engage with in life what values and goals we live for and what we expect for the future, in the short term and eternally. We can create a defined and written defense, but also need an extemporaneous sharing of what it means for us to have our hope in Jesus Christ for eternity. Such words of witness also have the help of God's Spirit in both our communication and in opening receptive minds and hearts in those we address.

In its simplest form, we bear witness to what we know and experience. We can do that as we talk about our families, homes, cars, clothes, vacations, and all sorts of subjects. I encourage you to use that same level of conversation to describe what it means to have God in your life. If you are asked or encouraged to express something deep that you need to prepare for, you can get back to people with your answer. You can also point them to other resources. There is no shortage of Christian material; we have huge numbers of books in print and vast amounts of information online.

We need people to take the truth and interpret it to neighbors and friends in language that is authentic. Personally, we need to communicate the beauty of living with hope in Jesus Christ now and forever. The world is full of people suffering and imprisoned in many forms of darkness. They are lost, hurting, living without Christ, and without hope. These people need the Lord, and God can use you to point them to the source of life and hope. Share what you know; tell about what you experience as a child of God.

PSALMS, HYMNS, AND SONGS

Psalm 69: My Song Forever Shall Record
I Serve a Living Savior
We Have Heard the Joyful Sound

MEDITATION AND PRAYER

- What did you notice in particular about this reading?
- Did this bring to mind any recent experience?
- Do I sense God prompting me to change or to do anything?
- I wonder . . .
- I thank God for . . .

PRAYER OF BLESSING

God of all wisdom and knowledge, thank you for revealing yourself to the world in Jesus. Illumine me and help me communicate to others this good hope that works in real life.
For Jesus's sake, amen.

We have learned about storytelling from our earliest days!

PURIFYING HOPE

1 John 3:1–3: See what great love the Father has lavished on us, that we should be called children of God! And that is what we are! The reason the world does not know us is that it did not know him. Dear friends, now we are children of God, and what we will be has not yet been made known. But we know that when Christ appears, we shall be like him, for we shall see him as he is. All who have this hope in him purify themselves, just as he is pure.

This passage talks about how, when our hope is fully realized, we shall become like Jesus forever. We will not equal him, but instead reflect his image. We are adopted already by grace through faith into God's family; we are privileged to now be children of God. Now we need to strive to be more like him in our lives. We remain unfinished and continue to be a work in process. But someday we shall bear his likeness completely. To get there will take effort on our part and transformative power on God's part.

Your efforts to overcome sin and your resolve to surrender fully to him are absolutely necessary. You are not a passive part in this critical work of sanctification. Yet God's efforts will be the greater part of this project. That too will demonstrate his lavish love. Such a beautiful word to describe his work—lavish! God doesn't sprinkle a few drops of love on you. He pours it out forever.

Because we have this hope in Jesus, the text tells us that we are purified. I think of this in terms of the lifelong work of sanctification, where God keeps developing Christ within us and demonstrating him to the world through us.

Think of a sculptor chiseling us out of a Carrara marble block. Chunks need to be removed of the old sinful nature; fine finish work needs to be done to polish our rough edges. I think also of how this is like the process of refining metal. There is a lot of dross to be removed and impurities to be taken out to be the pure quality needed to fill the mold of Jesus's shape. When it's all done, *"we shall be like Jesus, for we shall see him as he is."*

Praise God that he directs such a process in your life! His goal is that you become children perfectly able to fill your place around his heavenly banquet, and after partaking enjoy and marvel at the wonders in his perfect new creation.

PSALMS, HYMNS, AND SONGS

Psalm 66: O All Ye Peoples Bless Our God
Lord Jesus I Long To Be Perfectly Whole
O For a Closer Walk With God
Be Like Jesus, This My Song

MEDITATION AND PRAYER

- What did I notice in particular about this reading?
- Did this bring to mind any recent experiences?
- Do I sense God prompting me to change or to do anything?
- I wonder . . .
- I thank God for . . .

PRAYER OF BLESSING

Loving Father in heaven, may I cherish the privilege of being your child who has been given the promise that in the eternal future, together with all your children, I shall become like Jesus—all of which will be fully revealed at his return.
In Christ, amen

Modern blast furnace

LIVING HOPE

1 Peter 1:3–6 (read 1–11): Praise be to the God and Father of our Lord Jesus Christ! In his great mercy he has given us new birth into a living hope through the resurrection of Jesus Christ from the dead, and into an inheritance that can never perish, spoil or fade. This inheritance is kept in heaven for you, who through faith are shielded by God's power until the coming of the salvation that is ready to be revealed in the last time. In all this you, greatly rejoice, though now for a little while you may have had to suffer grief in all kinds of trials.

I love that Peter uses the adjective *living* here: We are born anew into a *living* hope. Peter was painfully aware of Jesus's death, but also his triumphant resurrection. This living Lord enables us to have a living hope, verdant and fruitful.

It's not a drab, grayscale concept, but one that keeps us alive on the inside and gives us eternal life when our mortal bodies are changed to be like his and we enjoy the inheritance that is ours in heaven. We live because he lives, we inherit because we are children of God, "co-heirs with Christ" as Scripture declares (Romans 8:16). As you ponder the life to come, make sure you embrace this *living* aspect rather than some lifeless idea of the future.

We shall be part of a new creation, more glorious than the one we are in right now. It will be full of life that reflects the glory of the Living God—Father, Son, and Holy Spirit with whom we will live and reign forever. The vitality and growth you shall experience will exceed all of your expectations, and you will be so fully alive that you will experience it with all your senses and your complete and perfected being.

The beauty awaiting us will be purged of sin and all its toxic effects. As John writes in Revelation 21:4–5, *"He will wipe every tear from their eyes. There will be no more death or mourning or crying or pain, for the old order of things has passed away."*

On this earth, says Peter, we may have to *"suffer grief in all kinds of trials."* Let this not be a hopeless suffering, but one that embraces the life and hope we have now in Christ and looks ahead to the glorious hope of all that we shall inherit with Jesus in his kingdom. Grace helps us through it all. Keep your eyes lifted up to God, who will make all things new.

PSALMS, HYMNS, AND SONGS

My Life Flows On In Endless Praise Forever

Because He Lives

Day by Day

The King Shall Come When the Morning Dawns

MEDITATION AND PRAYER

- What did I notice in particular about this reading?
- Did this bring to mind any recent experiences?
- Do I sense God prompting me to change or to do anything?
- I wonder . . .
- I thank God for . . .

PRAYER OF BLESSING

Eternal God, help me to hold dear the living hope that is established in the resurrection of Jesus Christ. Assure me of the inheritance that is waiting in heaven. Strengthen my faith daily with the work of the Holy Spirit. Through Christ, amen.

The Sonoran Desert in Arizona, one of my favorite places, has so much beauty and life, especially when it rains! It represents to me how we have a living hope even in tough places that feel like deserts.

RESURRECTION HOPE

1 Corinthians 15:19–20 (read 12–20): If only for this life we have hope in Christ, we are all people most to be pitied. But Christ has indeed been raised from the dead, the firstfruits of those who have fallen asleep.

If you want to saturate yourself in what God says about hope, you should read all of 1 Corinthians 15. I selected only a small part of this glorious chapter on the effects of the resurrection of Jesus Christ. The Easter Gospel is good news for our eternal future, assuring us that those who belong to Jesus will be raised, even as he was, from the dead. He was *"the firstfruits; then, when he comes, those who belong to him"* will also be raised (vs. 23).

We mortals need to grasp this truth tightly. We may deny or repress this reality, but I assure you it is true. One of the people I served as pastor and whose funeral I conducted used to tell me, "I have an expiration date." She spoke the truth. In the stark face of our mortality, the wonderful news of the gospel is that we will one day be raised from the dead.

This fact is the foundation of our hope for the life to come, and is assured by the fact that Jesus was raised first. If we fail to grasp what is going to happen, then we Christians are a bunch of losers, pitiful objects of ridicule. But our hope is in the living Lord Jesus Christ, who will raise us from the dead. Then we shall become imperishable and immortal, and bear the likeness of the risen Christ himself (as stated later in the chapter).

This is the culmination of the blessed hope that God gives us. We are not bound to this earth forever, nor does our hope lie here. While we have hope in the present, which enables us to keep moving forward to eternity, we are ultimately bound for glory.

This is the hope that sustains us when the end of our journey on earth comes near and we face death. This is the hope we hold when people we love dearly are called out of this life before us. When death occurs, Christ will usher us into eternal life, to the home he has prepared for us. We will personally experience the miraculous transformation of the resurrection of the dead. Wow, what will that be like?!

Wait in hope, for one day we shall joyfully and securely live forever in his kingdom. *"But thanks be to God! He gives us the victory through our Lord Jesus Christ"* (v. 57).

PSALMS, HYMNS, AND SONGS

The Day of Resurrection
I Know That My Redeemer Lives
Jesus Lives and So Shall I
For All the Saints

MEDITATION AND PRAYER

- What did I notice in particular about this reading?
- Did this bring to mind any recent experiences?
- Do I sense God prompting me to change or to do anything?
- I wonder . . .
- I thank God for . . .

PRAYER OF BLESSING

Eternal God, we rejoice in the victory of Jesus Christ. As I struggle with the challenges in this fallen world, let the Easter Gospel proclaim the defeat over sin and death and the sure hope that one day all of God's people will be raised with Christ to share your glory. In Christ, amen.

Vincent Van Gogh, *A Wheatfield with Cypresses*

This composition is rich in symbols with its wheat field, cypress and olive trees, mountains and sky. I think it portrays hope and resurrection (courtesy of Metropolitan Museum of Art, New York).

GOD IS LOVE!

1 John 4:7–11 (read 7–16): Dear Friends, let us love one another, for love comes from God. Everyone who loves has been born of God and knows God. Whoever does not love does not know God, because God is love. This is how God showed his love among us: He sent his one and only Son into the world that we might live through him. This is love: not that we loved God, but that he loved us and sent his Son as an atoning sacrifice for our sins. Dear friends, since God so loved us, we also ought to love one another.

Much has been written about love, but to truly understand it we need to look to the true source of love: God. He not only loves us, he is love. God embodies love as one of the essential attributes of his divine being. We cannot conceive of God apart from love, any more than we could know him apart from his holiness or other attributes. He is more than love, but He always loves.

We need to start with God, not with earthly primal urges, to know what love is. Sadly, love has become a confusing concept, with many expressions of it coming from "below." In these verses we see it revealed as coming from "above," from God.

As we read about love in 1 John 4, we discover right away that it is active and not self-centered. The energy that love generates is an outflowing love, a love that gives instead of takes. It reaches out to the one who is loved, rather than seeking first to receive. This will always distinguish God's authentic love from its counterfeits.

God-based love does not depend upon receiving love in return, although it is designed to be a gift that is mutually shared. But it is not designed to be an exact gift exchange. Love is simply given, yet when given to other believers it should be natural that we love back and our relationships grow.

Our human nature is depraved, so our responses may not always be God-based. More than that, human love can inflict deep pain. But that does not stop love from continuing its outward flow. It may call for care and appropriate boundaries on our parts to channel it, and we must be wise in these times. But the desire to protect love is strong so that it continues its outward flow.

May God's love continue to fill you and flow through you to one another and to people beyond your comfortable circle. What a privilege it is that God uses you to reflect His love to a world in such need of it.

PSALMS, HYMNS, AND SONGS

The Old Rugged Cross
Love Divine All Loves Excelling
Praise Him, Praise Him
Jesu, Jesu, Fill Us With Your Love
Lift High the Cross

MEDITATION AND PRAYER

- What did I notice in particular about this reading?
- Did this bring to mind any recent experiences?
- Do I sense God prompting me to change or to do anything?
- I wonder . . .
- I thank God for . . .

PRAYER OF BLESSING

God of grace, how privileged I am to know and experience that you are the God of love! May I be filled and refilled with your wonderful love, and may it also flow from me as a channel to others. In the name of Christ, who loved us and died for us, amen.

The Old Rugged Cross

ABIDING IN CHRIST AND HIS LOVE

John 15:1, 4–5 (read 1–16): I am the true vine, and my Father is the gardener . . . Remain in me, and I also remain in you. No branch can bear fruit by itself; it must remain in the vine. Neither can you bear fruit unless you remain in me. I am the vine; you are the branches. If you remain in me and I in you, you will bear much fruit; apart from me you can do nothing.

When we are closely connected to Jesus as the source of life, we discover that he is also the source of our love and gives us the ability to authentically love and serve. This glorifies him and is also the fruit that he expects from us. He has great expectations for us and wants us to be abundant in love and service to one another and to the world.

This love starts just outside of our doors and reaches across the globe. "Remaining," or as it is translated in some versions "abiding in Christ," sustains us. Sometimes we go through difficult growing seasons, yet we continue forward as long as we keep our vital lifeline to Jesus open. When we by willful action or neglect restrict that lifeline, we cut ourselves off from the source of life. We wither and are in danger of failure.

When your "love crop" is under stress, be sure you hear loud and clear the warning of Jesus that "apart from me you can do nothing." Remain in him, return to him; the alternative is to be chopped off from the source of life.

Your life when connected to Jesus by faith, regularly expressed and nurtured, becomes a blessing to many. Each day take the time to maintain the flow of life with study of his Word, meditation, and prayer. Worship God in the community of his church, make moments during your day to pause and adore him. You will better enjoy your Christian life if you do, for you will feel spiritually vibrant and healthy.

In addition to personal growth, others will receive the love of Christ through you and this can prompt them to develop the fruit of grateful loving service in their lives. This multiplies God's love starting with you and spreading to Christians all over the world. The world is blessed when the love of God in Christ is spread.

The world has a long way to go and resistance is strong. But God is Almighty, Jesus is the Victorious Lord, and the kingdom comes as his powerful love is expressed through you and me. By remaining in him all things are possible.

PSALMS, HYMNS, AND SONGS

Now I Belong To Jesus

I Am His and He Is Mine

Blessed Assurance

MEDITATION AND PRAYER

- What did I notice in particular about this reading?
- Did this bring to mind any recent experiences?
- Do I sense God prompting me to change or to do anything?
- I wonder . . .
- I thank God for . . .

PRAYER OF BLESSING

Loving God, as many forces seek to separate me from you, direct all your gracious resources to hold me close. Assist me to respond fully and joyfully to your divine embrace. In this abiding, may all the fruitful responses that develop glorify you. For Christ's sake, amen.

Fall grape harvest at Chateau Chantal Winery on Mission Peninsula in Michigan (courtesy of Kyle Brownley, Chateau Chantal Winery and Inn).

THE SUPREME MODEL OF LOVE

John 3:16–18 (read 11–21): For God so loved the world that he gave his one and only Son, that whoever believes in him shall not perish but have eternal life. For God did not send his Son into the world to condemn the world, but to save the world through him. Whoever believes in him is not condemned, but whoever does not believe stands condemned already because they have not believed in the name of God's one and only Son.

The eloquence of these words should speak Good News to everyone who hears them! The clarity and simplicity of the Gospel are clear, revealing to us how God, who is love, loved the world so much that he gave his best to save it. He gave his one and only Son, and the four Gospels (Matthew, Mark, Luke, John) reveal the details from his holy conception to his crucifixion, burial, and resurrection.

Cumulatively, the Gospels reveal the investment God made to redeem the world. Personally, they tell every one of us who believe that we will not perish in judgement but live in the fullness of the love of God forever. The emphasis is fully on the Good News of Jesus. Yet there is also explicit warning about the consequences of rejecting this divine love.

I pray that you believe in Jesus as your Savior and know the assurance that comes with this. On one hand, this belief spares us from fear of condemnation by God. On the other it is our invitation to live in communion with God, enjoying his love and looking forward to even fuller manifestations of what it means to be God's beloved children. Jesus has a unique place as eternal Son, one with the Father and the Spirit. But we are also embraced as God's sons and daughters, cherished by him forever.

Saying any more may take away from the eloquence and clarity of this precious Gospel verse. Volumes have already been written about every aspect of this beloved passage, which you may want to explore. Today, however, take extra time, right now, to contemplate what this verse means. Don't move on until you have let this timeless truth saturate your mind and heart.

Don't gloss over it quickly! Savor it like you would the tastiest morsel you have been craving—take it in slowly and be filled with his goodness!

> God so loved the world that he gave his one and only Son,
> So as *I* believe in him, *I* shall not perish but have eternal life!

PSALMS, HYMNS, AND SONGS

For God So Loved the World
Love Lifted Me
Amazing Grace
And Can It Be That I Should Gain
The Old Rugged Cross

MEDITATION AND PRAYER

- What did I notice in particular about this reading?
- Did this bring to mind any recent experiences?
- Do I sense God prompting me to change or to do anything?
- I wonder . . .
- I thank God for . . .

PRAYER OF BLESSING

God of love and mercy, impress upon me how great and wondrous your love is in my life, and also to the fallen world that Jesus came to save. May my response develop and deepen, and your love be always treasured. For Jesus's sake, amen.

Engraving by Albrecht Durer (1508) (courtesy of Metropolitan Museum of Art, New York)

THE FULL EXTENT OF JESUS'S LOVE

John 13:1 (read 12:44–13:2): It was just before the Passover Festival. Jesus knew that the hour had come for him to leave this world and go to the Father. Having loved his own who were in the world, he loved them to the end.

How far did Jesus go to redeem you? He went from heaven to hell—from the glories of his eternal home to the agony and abandonment of the Cross. He went from everlasting life to death at Calvary. The evangelist John expresses it so sublimely: "He now showed them the full extent of his love" (RSV).

The RSV, another translation I love, also says, "Jesus loved them to the end." He did everything it took to save those he loved, those he called "his own." I like to add, "his own beloved ones, his own cherished ones."

What he accomplished is unfathomable and we have no adequate way to measure it. But know that what he did is HUGE. There is nothing comparable to what he selflessly did for us. It is divine work that God initiated out of love to save those he loves. Jesus's sacrifice was foreshadowed in the Passover Lamb during the exodus from Egypt long before, but now the beloved Son of God became a sacrifice to cover our sin and guilt. He became the Lamb of God.

When I try to stretch my comprehension of the vast extent of Christ's love, I appreciate it more when I confess how vast my own sinfulness really is. I can gloss over my sins easily, but when I am really honest before God and transparent to self, I know my failings. Confession truly is good for the soul. Through it I've discovered a greater awareness of how far Jesus went for me. I highly recommend such thinking yourself.

Finally, how much love should we give in turn to Jesus? How about the very most, expressed in a lifetime of adoration and service! Even our best could not match his loving sacrifice, but offering it demonstrates our grateful response to him. His love enables us to love as he loved us, right to the very end. We need to complete what we start, as he faithfully modeled for us. One day our imperfect efforts will be transformed and become faultless, and then we shall love him purely forever and ever with no end!

PSALMS, HYMNS, AND SONGS

And Can It Be
Jesus Paid It All
All the Way My Savior Leads Me
He Who Began A Good Work In You

MEDITATION AND PRAYER

- What did I notice in particular about this reading?
- Did this bring to mind any recent experiences?
- Do I sense God prompting me to change or to do anything?
- I wonder . . .
- I thank God for . . .

PRAYER OF BLESSING

Father, impress upon me the extent of Jesus's sacrifice and the immensity of his work. Keep this from becoming merely familiar words, and let this lead to unending love and service unto the exalted Lord Jesus, in whose blessed name we pray. Amen.

The passage below has been called the Kenosis passage, after a Greek word which is translated variously as "made himself nothing," "emptied," but also "poured out." The classic clay vessel below, used in first century and many others, can assist you in considering how Christ poured himself out of his heavenly glory to become like you and die in your place. To whom are you pouring yourself out in humble service?

PHILIPPIANS 2:5–11

Your attitude should be the same as that of Christ Jesus:

Who, being in very nature God, did not consider equality with God something to be grasped,but made himself nothing, taking the very nature of a servant, being made in human likeness. And being found in appearance as a man, he humbled himself and became obedient to death—even death on a cross! Therefore God exalted him to the highest place and gave him the name that is above every name, that at the name of Jesus every knee should bow, in heaven and on earth and under the earth,and every tongue confess that Jesus Christ is Lord, to the glory of God the Father.

JESUS'S NEW COMMAND

John 13:34–35: "A new command I give you: Love one another. As I have loved you, so you must love one another. By this everyone will know that you are my disciples, if you love one another."

Because God is love and because he so loved the world that he gave his Son, his plan is that those who believe in the Son will form a community based on love. This is what Jesus says to the disciples, and is the plan for the church in all its manifestations. Sounds easy enough, right? The reality is that creating a loving community was a constant challenge for the Twelve, just as it is for us.

Our selfish and fallen natures work against this plan. Sometimes we are so self-absorbed that we are blindly unaware of the effect we have on others. Communication is such a complex process that we can easily misunderstand one another. We take offense when offense was never intended.

At times we wrestle with our motivation, vacillating between "have to" and "want to." Christ declares we *need to* love one another. People fail us, which leads to hurt and causes us to hold back and even actively shun others. We can create excuses and mentally justify our supposedly righteous actions. In hard times, we can despair of the possibility for authentic, shared love and decide to just take care of ourselves.

However, the new command to love remains in force and it doesn't have exclusion clauses. Love expects that we will forgive one another as we have been forgiven by our Savior. "Love one another" is always Christ's command to all who follow him. It is a work requirement for everyone who seeks employment in his kingdom of love and grace!

To truly love, we must work through the obstacles within us along with those the evil one puts before us in subtle ways. The way forward is to understand the love Jesus commands us to have and which he models for us. It is known as *agapic* love, after the Greek word in the original Scripture. Jesus's love is distinguished from its dim reflections and plastic imitations in a world disconnected from Christ.

As your bond with Jesus remains strong, your love will be recharged by his divine love and it will flow out through you. This love gives without expectation of reciprocal response, even flowing when faced with rejection.

This love showcases Christ in us, and it is an example to those who are lost of what they need more than anything else! Their need for Christ may be repressed, but that need can also illuminate their deep darkness and lead them to Christ.

PSALMS, HYMNS, AND SONGS

Psalm 138: How Good and Pleasant Is The Sight

Christian Hearts in Love United

They'll Know We Are Christians By Our Love

I Love You with The Love of The Lord

MEDITATION AND PRAYER

- What did I notice in particular about this reading?
- Did this bring to mind any recent experiences?
- Do I sense God prompting me to change or to do anything?
- I wonder . . .
- I thank God for . . .

PRAYER OF BLESSING

Father, we keep looking to Jesus to learn about true love for one another in this broken and jagged world. Help us to authentically love one another, and in my life and those within my circles of influence, let this love be a testimony to the love of Jesus, in whose name we pray, amen.

John the Beloved, in a stained glass portrayal of the Last Supper, (courtesy of The Church of the Holy Trinity, New York).

STRETCHING OUR LOVE

Matthew 5:43–48: "You have heard that it was said, 'Love your neighbor and hate your enemy.' But I tell you, love your enemies and pray for those who persecute you, that you may be children of your Father in heaven. He causes his sun to rise on the evil and the good, and sends rain on the righteous and the unrighteous. If you love those who love you, what reward will you get? Are not even the tax collectors doing that? And if you greet only your brothers, what are you doing more than others? Do not even pagans do that? Be perfect, therefore, as your heavenly Father is perfect."

God has lavishly poured out his love for us via Christ. Why is it that we limit its flow through us into others? Is there some unholy self-righteousness at work in our hearts that, together with pride, allows us to judge who is worthy and who is not?

I think that explains a lot of what happens to Jesus's followers. Our anxieties about strangers, which parents instilled in childhood through their warnings, has also affected us. Jesus addresses this fear early in his public ministry.

There is of course something natural about liking "our kind of people." We are comfortable with familiar faces. We are less threatened and more secure with people like us, while also acknowledging that there are dangerous predators and fraudulent people lurking in our neighborhoods and electronic media. There are real enemies that would like to harm us. Being careful and guarding appropriate boundaries are necessary today. It is building insurmountable walls between "us" and "them" that Jesus addresses.

Jesus calls us to transcend the comfort of liking our "own kind of people" into practicing "his kind of love." He urges us to get beyond our comfort zones to show his love everywhere, even to people we fear such as those who persecute us. We need to reach "God's kind of people," many of whom are lost. He urges us to show his kind of love and thereby demonstrate that we are his children.

As Christ's love flows through us, we are to spread it broadly and indiscriminately. Many people do favors for others, not just because they like them but because they want to influence them or get something in return. Christ's love doesn't have such expectations. It is designed to demonstrate his love through us, to lead people to life in him. It is truly a gift, not a gift exchange!

PSALMS, HYMNS, AND SONGS

In Christ There Is No East or West

They'll Know We Are Christians by Our Love

We Are God's People

MEDITATION AND PRAYER

- What did I notice in particular about this reading?
- Did this bring to mind any recent experiences?
- Do I sense God prompting me to change or to do something?
- I wonder . . .
- I thank God for . . .

PRAYER OF BLESSING

God of love and grace, work in me to demonstrate to those around me your love through Christ our Lord. Challenge me to channel Christ's love more broadly, to press my existing boundaries and love unconditionally, freed from self-righteousness. For Jesus's sake, amen.

God's kind of people?

ORDERING OUR LOVES

Matthew 22:36–40: [The lawyer asked,] "Teacher, which is the greatest commandment in the Law?" Jesus replied: "'Love the Lord your God with all your heart and with all your soul and with all your mind.' This is the first and greatest commandment. And the second is like it: 'Love your neighbor as yourself.' All the Law and the Prophets hang on these two commandments."

Jesus's words here are a beautiful summary of the Ten Commandments, which are at the heart of the Old Testament message given in the Law and Prophets. We have noted how God himself is love, and that it is a natural expectation we will love him in return and share it with others. Often we speak of this as our grateful response to the saving love of God—which he initiates and which we embrace by faith in Jesus.

The priority for our love almost goes without saying: the first and highest goes to God. We offer our highest commitment, all of our heart, soul, and mind. Knowing this begs for personal assessment—are you offering your all, or some fraction thereof? Jesus's expectations in this text are very clear.

The flow of love is also directed to others, to our neighbors. Some are close to us, and we have made vows and commitments to them before God that need to be honored. We want to honor them! But we also reach out to others in and outside of our comfort zones. We care about them, offering acceptance and service to those who are in need. When we look at needs on a world-wide scale, it overwhelms us. But prayer for guidance can narrow our focus to those whom God would have us express love.

Easily overlooked in this text is the place for self-love. I know love for self and others requires balance, but I believe the issue needs to be addressed. Some people err on the side of too much self-love, leading to selfishness and cutting off the flow of love to others. Narcissism is a snare for many. On the other extreme is neglect of self, and self-abuse can result. We were not made for pure self-indulgence, yet God surrounds us with blessings in his creation to enjoy as faithful stewards.

In balance, we are to care for our needs and our health as God's children who value ourselves, but don't seek to worship self. Pray for wisdom in the balance and ordering of your love to God, others, and self. May you establish a grace-based, balanced self-esteem as daughters and sons of God.

PSALMS, HYMNS, AND SONGS

Father, I Adore You
My God How Wonderful Thou Art
More Love To Thee, O Christ

MEDITATION AND PRAYER

- What did I notice in particular about this reading?
- Did this bring to mind any recent experiences?
- Do I sense God prompting me to change or to do anything?
- I wonder . . .
- I thank God for . . .

PRAYER OF BLESSING

God of glory, help me to love you above all, and find balance in the other directions love takes. Guard me from loving this world apart from you. Guide me in self-care but keep me from inordinate self-love. Grant wisdom, for Christ's sake, amen.

God, who is love, embraces us with his greatest love, so we can grow in love for others, and also ourselves.

DAY 34

THE PAYMENT OF LOVE

Romans 13:8–9 (read 8–10): Let no debt remain outstanding, except the continuing debt to love one another, for whoever loves others has fulfilled the law. The commandments, "You shall not commit adultery," "You shall not murder," "You shall not steal," "You shall not covet," and whatever other command there may be, are summed up in this one command. "Love your neighbor as yourself."

The context of these verses indicates that the words apply to "neighbor love," and to fulfill them according to God's desire means far more than the "do not" side of the Ten Commandments. For example, I may not have murdered my neighbor but I may not have loved him or her either. When I care for my neighbor by assisting if there are unmet needs, looking out for my neighbor if they are mistreated, and treating them with respect and kindness—then I am loving my neighbor.

The apostle Paul puts the rule to "Love your neighbor as yourself" in language that implies we owe that love to our neighbor. In the broader chapter he describes fitting responses to government authorities and civic duties, calling for honor and obedience. As the chapter flows into our text, he presents neighbor love as our appropriate response as God's people. We humble ourselves to meet their needs before many of our needs in ways that our conscience and the Christian community determine is fitting in each circumstance.

Few people in America like to think that they owe their neighbor much, if anything at all. Yet we have abundant opportunity to show that we have Christian values and God's love, which guide the way we consider our neighbor and our responses to them.

I have come to the conclusion, after decades of ministry, that everyone has needs and hurts hidden within that need attention. Many needs are buried under a facade of bravado, many are silently borne, and many are so deeply repressed that the individual is unaware of them.

Love is an agent of healing and help. When we selflessly share Christ's love, a powerful message about him and a tangible remedy is offered. We need love from the first day of our lives to the last. Give thanks for the love you receive; give love to those who are without it!

PSALMS, HYMNS, AND SONGS

I Will Tell The Wondrous Story

Jesus Paid It All

The Servant Song

MEDITATION AND PRAYER

- What did I notice in particular about this reading?
- Did this bring to mind any recent experiences?
- Do I sense God prompting me to change or to do anything?
- I wonder . . .
- I thank God for . . .

PRAYER OF BLESSING

God of mercy, we cannot repay you for your grace to us. We marvel that it was freely given. Thank you! Yet we can respond in gratitude to you, and also meet the needs of others. Prompt me to demonstrate neighbor love which reflects the love of Christ, in whose blessed name we pray, amen.

LOVE'S RESTORATIVE WORK

1 Peter 4:8: Above all, love each other deeply,
because love covers over a multitude of sins.

I have done a good many restoration projects over the years. I have repaired rust on my cars, restored old oak furniture, patched and painted or papered walls. I have restored my flooded basement with help from a restoration company, and discovered that this is a large industry. With the effects of aging, plus the consequence of accidents, fires, and natural disasters, there is regularly a lot of restoration work to be done in and around houses.

In our relationships with others, there is also a lot of restoration work to be done. Our hurtful words, in league with anger or envy, do much damage. Unforgiving spirits leave their marks in the hearts of others. Spirits are crushed by ridicule or withering criticism. The reality is that even precious children are able to inflict hurt on others, with this malign skill set developing as we mature.

Unless and until our hearts are rehabilitated, the damage will continue. By letting go of our anger and other sins in confession, coupled with a desire to let the renewing love of Christ control us, we discover we are on the path to loving one another as we have been loved.

The wonder of grace begins to show up in our relationships, and we discover that love is able to repair the damage sin inflicted. Grace enables us to lay down our conflicts and fix the cracks with restorative words and deeds. We can then give the relationship a fresh look, like when applying a new coat of paint. We know there was damage covered over, but we let it go and let it vanish from our working memory.

This requires forgiveness and reconciliation, and still may need a little touchup now and then. We choose to let the past go and welcome the current relationship.

This is how God looks at us. It is the foundation of the doctrine of justification by faith, which teaches us how we have the covering of Christ's righteousness over our broken and sinful lives. Christ's righteousness covers our guilt and comes about through our union with Christ by faith. God chooses to see our new selves, the self being renewed after the image of Christ.

May God give you a grateful heart that embraces his forgiving work, modeling that forgiveness in your relationships. May your love be willing to lay aside the past, initiate restoration, and work together for a better tomorrow.

PSALM, HYMNS, AND SONGS

Forgive Our Sins As We Forgive
Lord I Want to Be A Christian In My Heart
Jesu, Jesu, Fill Us with Your Love

MEDITATION AND PRAYER

- What did I notice in particular about this reading?
- Did this bring to mind any recent experiences?
- Do I sense God prompting me to change or to do anything?
- I wonder . . .
- I thank God for . . .

PRAYER OF BLESSING

God of love, we give thanks that practicing the love shown us in Jesus enables us to forgive one another and restore frayed relationships. Conflict and hurt grow so quickly, but let me show this restorative and edifying love to others. After the example of Jesus, in whom we pray, amen.

Restoration tools!

SPEAKING THE TRUTH IN LOVE

Ephesians 4:14–16: Then we will no longer be infants, tossed back and forth by the waves, and blown here and there by every wind of teaching and by the cunning and craftiness of people in their deceitful scheming. Instead, speaking the truth in love, we will grow to become In every respect the mature body of him who is the head, that is, Christ. From him the whole body, joined and held together by every supporting ligament, grows and builds itself up in love, as each part does its work.

As I read these verses, it struck me that the apostle Paul was facing an assault on truth very similar to our current context. Truth liberates and lies enslave; at their deepest levels they flow from our Father in heaven or the father of lies below. The power of corruptive persuasion goes back to the Garden of Eden, and is now amplified through our modern media globally and almost instantly.

Truth can be distorted to sound like lies, and vice versa. Truth affects what we believe and how we live; it can enhance our value system and our ethics, while lies can corrode them. I take comfort in knowing that the early church, quickly beset by heresy and false prophets, prevailed and prized the truth. That truth is still revealed and available to us. God continues to give discernment to us through his Spirit as we walk in the way of Jesus Christ, who is Truth (John 14:6) and also the embodiment of love.

In this age of relative and alternative truths, we are called to speak the truth in love. Doing so is a sign of our spiritual maturity and demonstrates our ability to discern what we hear and wisely communicate what needs to be said.

As we grow in our relationship with Christ, it becomes natural that we express truth in love. Truth is woven into how we express ourselves, as well as the many subtle messages we give non-verbally. Our default mode of communication is not designed to distort or hurt. Some of what we hear and read is unfortunately directed towards divisive and destructive ends by people with evil-based persuasive abilities.

God blesses those who attempt in private conversations and also in the public arena to speak truth in love. We do so courageously even when hard truths must be brought into the light. Love does not deny facts, but seeks to present them with integrity and not as a weapon.

Truth in love builds up another person, creates respect, and can open the way for reconciliation. Every day, before we open our mouths, we need to not only engage our brain but our loving hearts as well. As we do we can glorify God, the source of all truth, and bless those who hear the truth in love.

PSALMS, HYMNS, AND SONGS

O Speak To Me That I May Speak
Love In Any Language
Thy Word
O Be Careful Little Tongue

MEDITATION AND PRAYER

- What did I notice in particular about this reading?
- Did this bring to mind any recent experiences?
- Do I sense God prompting me to change or to do anything?
- I wonder . . .
- I thank God for . . .

PRAYER OF BLESSING

Our Father, you made us in your image and equipped us with so many abilities. Our ability to communicate is a blessing for communion with you and communication with one another. Yet our fallen nature distorts it, and we are easily divided. Use me to counter this, and to speak the truth in love boldly and faithfully. For Jesus's sake, amen.

We need to filter our mouths for many reasons!

ROOTED FIRMLY IN CHRIST

Ephesians 3:17b–19 (read 14–21): And I pray that you, being rooted and established in love, may have power, together with all the Lord's holy people, to grasp how wide and long and high and deep is the love of Christ, and to know that love which surpasses knowledge—that you may be filled to the measure of all the fullness of God.

These verses are part of an elegant prayer that I encourage you to read later in its entirety in verses 14–21. I focus here on the fact that you have deep roots in love, that *agapic* love that you have from Christ. Faith is planted as a seed in your heart and needs roots that go deep and keep growing. As the superstructure of your life catches the strong winds and storms, it is easy to be shaken. Without deep and wide roots, you will be toppled. When you are rooted in Christ you are in the bedrock that your soul needs, and your love will be secure!

As you are filled with love via those deep roots, you are commanded to go out and use that love. It is like energy in your tank to share with others. We all need regular refills, but this source is unlimited. We never need to worry that if we give too much away we will run out. Instead, the more we give the more we receive in the economics in Christ's kingdom.

As you are filled with love, you will also discover that you are filled with the indwelling Christ. "*You will be filled to the measure of all the fullness of God*," as the text states. You don't have the capacity to contain all that, but Christ enlarges you and your capacity will grow. As you reflect on the text above, I challenge you to think larger than you ever have before. Stretch yourself completely!

How do you grasp the dimensions of the love of Christ? Begin by realizing how much you have received of its width and length, height and depth. Consider how much you never noticed but took for granted. Look beyond yourself to those you care about and consider what they have received. Go as far as you can imagine in ever-increasing concentric circles, trying to grasp what Christ has done for all of his people over the earth and over the ages. That's a big stretch. How far can you reach?

PSALMS, HYMNS, AND SONGS

I Have Decided to Follow Jesus
In Christ Alone
Jesus Priceless Treasure
Man of Sorrows

MEDITATION AND PRAYER

- What did I notice in particular about this reading?
- Did this bring to mind any recent experiences?
- Do I sense God prompting me to change or to do anything?
- I wonder . . .
- I thank God for . . .

PRAYER OF BLESSING

O God, you are awesome and your majesty surrounds us in creation. Your amazing love also surrounds us, and we experience it yet never comprehend it all. Thank you for what I already know of it, and fill me even more fully in all the days to come until we all experience the ultimate expression in glory forever. In Christ, amen.

Yellowstone Canyon from the top of Lower Falls in Yellowstone National Park. The vista, depth, expanse, and rich colors, including the rainbow on the lower left, remind me of the text in Ephesians 3:17b–19.

THE ATTRIBUTES OF LOVE

1 Corinthians 13:4–8a (read 1–13): Love is patient, love is kind. It does not envy, it does not boast, it is not proud. It does not dishonor others, it is not self-seeking, it is not easily angered, it keeps no record of wrongs. Love does not delight in evil but rejoices with the truth. It always protects, always trusts, always hopes, always perseveres. Love never fails.

What does love in action and attitude look like on ground level where you live? We have the inspired words above as tangible examples of what the love of Christ looks like. You have the opportunity to practice these examples daily. This doesn't exhaust the possibilities, but opens our hearts and minds to how we take a divine gift and share it with others.

If all of God's people faithfully expressed this kind of practical love, the world would be transformed. If we couple this love with the words of our Lord himself in the Golden Rule, our problems between neighbors and nations would disappear.

"So in everything, do unto others what you would have them do unto you" (Matt. 7:12). I remind you of the New Command, *"Love one another as I have loved you,"* and invite you to think about how your world could improve as you practice these faithfully—and how the world will know our Savior by such love.

This kind of love is countercultural. People whose goal is power and money will scoff and take advantage of those who practice such Christ-like actions. They are takers, not givers. The truth is that love is so powerful that the evil one works desperately hard to ruin the work of love, perverting all that he can.

But the powers of hell can no better destroy Christ's love than they could destroy him on the cross. His Church too will prevail. He will continue to channel his love through you, and through his church on earth. Christ will work his purpose out. Leave the results up to him!

The verses quoted above end with, *"Love never fails."* God's purposes will continue. At times we may stumble, and at other times it seems the love we give has no effect. It is not pleasant to have it rejected. Yet love continues on, flowing from its source. Love will, in actions and words, always follow the example of our Lord, as we studied in Day 30: *"He loved us to the end."* Praise the Lord!

PSALMS, HYMNS, AND SONGS

Love in Any Language
Jesu, Jesu, Fill Us With Your Love
More Like The Master

MEDITATION AND PRAYER

- What did I notice in particular about this reading?
- Did this bring to mind any recent experiences?
- Do I sense God prompting me to change or to do anything?
- I wonder . . .
- I thank God for . . .

PRAYER OF BLESSING

God of grace, you have acted favorably toward us! Your acts are many and wondrous, and the saving work of Jesus, whom you sent into this fallen world, is central to them all. As I am loved, may that energize me for countless expressions of love as modeled by Jesus, in whom we pray, amen.

© JEN NORTON ART STUDIO

THE SYNERGY OF FAITH, HOPE, AND LOVE

1 Thessalonians 1:2–3: We always thank God for all of you and continually mention you in our prayers. We remember before our God and Father your work produced by faith, your labor prompted by love, and your endurance inspired by hope in our Lord Jesus Christ.

We have been studying the nature of faith, hope, and love for the past thirty-six chapters. An even dozen each! But they have no partition walls between them in living out the Christian life. The three are dynamically engaged and work in part and as a whole through your adventure in the wilderness of life. They build on one another in ways easily recognized, but also in ways beyond our awareness.

I strongly believe that all three of these gifts need to be used. If one remains inactive, you will not thrive and your balance will be off for your life journey. They are like a three-cylinder engine: each one is essential.

As we engage with faith, hope, and love, they lead to good work for God's kingdom. The apostle Paul prays with thanksgiving for what he knew was happening in the struggling new church in Thessalonica. He particularly recognized the power of faith, love, and hope in their community, and the fruit they developed in the people. The new believers were sustained by that fruit, and would be into the future.

We noted in our study for Day 2 how these three are the first things mentioned in the guidance and encouragement given to the Colossian believers. The letters Paul wrote (the epistles) needed to be fairly short, so the inclusion of these expressions shows how important they are for Christian living. My prayer is that your understanding and esteem for them has grown through your use of the devotions in this book.

Faith, hope, and love are given by the Lord to sustain you well until the end of your life and life as we know it here on Earth. Not one should be missing in your life! When Jesus comes to usher us into his Kingdom, the faith in the unseen we have needed will fall away because we will be with him face to face. The hope that we have held through life becomes the new reality we enter.

But love remains forever, and that perfect love will be ours to express to our Lord and his world family gathered with him at the end of days. "So now faith, hope, and love remain. But the greatest is love," the Bible says. Love is greatest and it lasts forever because it comes from the very being of God, who is love!

PSALMS, HYMNS, AND SONGS

Make Me A Channel Of Your Peace
Take My Life And Let It Be
More Like The Master
O Love That Will Not Let Me Go

MEDITATION AND PRAYER

- What did I notice in particular about this reading?
- Did this bring to mind any recent experiences?
- Do I sense God prompting me to change or to do anything?
- I wonder . . .
- I thank God for . . .

PRAYER OF BLESSING

O God my Shepherd, lead me along the path of life and provide all I need until the end. Bless me through all the gifts of your grace in Christ, including faith, hope, and love. May I live a life fruitful for your Kingdom, and one that brings glory to you, for Jesus's sake, amen.

As a gardener and farm market shopper I appreciate the continual effort it took to raise these foods for market—so with results produced by faith, hope, and love.

DAY 40

EQUIPPED FOR THE JOURNEY

1 Thessalonians 5:7–9 (read 1–11): For those who sleep, sleep at night, and those who get drunk, get drunk at night. But since we belong to the day, let us be sober, putting on faith and love as a breastplate, and the hope of salvation as a helmet. For God did not appoint us to suffer wrath but to receive salvation through our Lord Jesus Christ.

Today we conclude our study of how to be sustained in the wilderness times of life, which may last forty hours or forty years—or a lifetime. We face many challenges and trials in this wonderful yet perplexing thing called life. We are vulnerable to so many things that might overwhelm us. On our own we will be undone.

But thanks be to God! We have divine resources to help us daily and sustain us to the end. The gifts of faith, hope, and love work individually and together with great effect and synergy in our lives. The apostle Paul describes them in the text above as protective armor for trials and conflicts. They are effective in defense as well as offense, helping us persevere and also confront the darkness of evil.

The text also speaks of being self-controlled. Some translations use the word *sober,* which I prefer here because the text contrasts those who are self-controlled to people who are drunk in their darkness. Wallowing in darkness is their sad response to life's challenges.

What a glorious alternative you have! With divine help, you can be self-controlled as you use God's gifts of faith, hope, and love. Be sure you attend to them and keep your armor in good condition. Do not neglect to equip yourself daily, for you are not invincible. Give no space to pride, to deluding yourself into thinking you can handle the challenges alone. Our Lord will lead you to victory, and you are wise to follow Him faithfully and listen to his instructions.

While the spiritual armor you have is important for protection, it also equips you to face evil. There are many forms of spiritual darkness you will confront in this world. Faith, hope, and love not only sustain you—they are also powerful agents of change in others' lives. Never minimize the changes in life, family, and community that can occur when people come to faith in Christ, possess true hope, and learn what true love is.

Nations that put their faith in God, that have their hope in him, and who follow the practice of love that leads to justice will be richly blessed. This can be transformative and turn this fallen, upside-down world right side up—one person at a time, one community at a time.

Finally, God's goal for all described as *"belonging to the day"* is that they receive complete and eternal salvation! They shall have eternal life in the presence of God, enjoying Him, his people, and a new creation forever. What a glorious day that will be when God's goals are completed. AMEN!
Soli Deo Gloria

PSALMS, HYMNS, AND SONGS

Psalm 110: The Lord Unto His Christ Has Said

Lead On O King Eternal

The King Shall Come When Morning Dawns

Lead Me, Guide Me

MEDITATION AND PRAYER

- What did I notice in particular about this reading?
- Did this bring to mind any recent experiences?
- Do I sense God prompting me to change or to do anything?
- I wonder . . .
- I thank God for . . .

PRAYER OF BLESSING

Guide me, Almighty God,
as my pilgrimage continues
until I arrive at the destination
toward which Christ is leading
me. Let the armor of faith,
hope, and love protect me on
the journey and keep me strong
in my struggle against evil. In
Christ's strong name, amen.

An example of a
Roman Soldier in Armor.

POSTSCRIPT

One of my earliest childhood memories is walking on a forest trail with my dad on a spring day. He pointed out ferns emerging from the forest floor, calling them "fiddle-heads." He had to explain the meaning of that to me, and he described how they unfurl to reach their full potential. I was amazed, remembering the lesson, and to this day I enjoy growing many fern varieties in my garden. Several have been transplanted from one home to the next over our many moves. One of my garden favorites is pictured below—emerging and then developed—and it is called a Christmas Fern. It develops long, balanced fronds that stay green through much of the winter. It likely derived its common name from this evergreen-like feature (which sounds more inviting to me than its scientific name, *Polystichum acrostichoides!*).

I still enjoy observing my ferns unfurl in the springtime. I share this as it reminds me of how spiritual things grow in God's kingdom. Many things unfold and often take more time than we would prefer. Even Christ, to whom the Christmas Fern can point, came as God incarnate, yet was born as a helpless baby. Over time, he grew in stature, completed his redeeming work on earth, and returned to heaven. Now we live under his everlasting reign as Lord and Savior.

Under his care my experiences and understanding of faith, hope, and love have come a long way. This came about through study as well as my personal forays into the wilderness. I also learned much by ministering to others in such places, many of whom also ministered reciprocally to me. I hope in your growing seasons that faith, hope, and love will also unfurl nicely. I pray this book has assisted you and helps you be sustained on your way toward your eternal home with God.

WILDERNESS ADVENTURES

We noted at the beginning of this volume how wilderness can be a place of renewal and adventure. Yet these devotions focused on how we can find our way through the tough and uncharted seasons of life, which we sometimes call our wilderness places. At times it feels as though we are scarcely surviving. Yet that can be too stark a portrayal, for we can discover great blessings in our trials. Very often these become the places where we grow most deeply in our spiritual life. We draw close to the source of our life, the Triune God, discovering he is present in our wilderness places. These experiences can be framed as adventures with God, places where we don't just survive but thrive!

But the challenges of tough seasons can also deplete us. Thus we have the need for renewal, which God provides in many ways. The psalmist David expresses this in Psalm 23:1–3, "The Lord is my shepherd, I shall not want. He makes me lie down in green pastures, he leads me beside quiet waters, he restores my soul." Our Lord Jesus also encouraged us by example and teaching to "Come with me by yourselves to a quiet place and get some rest" (Mark 6:31). He taught us as well about prayer in an inner room or closet. Going to the Lord's house of prayer was part of his pattern.

Whether at home, briefly away for hours, or far off in a wilderness place, we do need times for renewal. Finding solitude is vital, and yet, without effort, hard to experience in our noisy, fast-paced world. Get unplugged and even use ear protectors if necessary! Many desire physical exercise and active adventures as well. Discover what works for you. Thankfully, opportunities are abundant for you to make plans for your personal renewal and replenishment. It may be in your home or your yard. It comes for many somewhere in the outdoors, and in wilderness places. The quiet waters pictured below are in Yellowstone National Park. There are many local, county, state, and national parks that you can enjoy. Be wise; put times and places on your schedule where you can be restored by God.

APPENDIX

BIBLE TEXTS FROM THE KING JAMES VERSION

DAY 1

1 Corinthians 13:13: And now abideth faith, hope, charity, these three; but the greatest of these is charity.

DAY 2

Colossians 1:3–5: We give thanks to God and the Father of our Lord Jesus Christ, praying always for you, Since we heard of your faith in Christ Jesus, and of the love which ye have to all the saints, For the hope which is laid up for you in heaven, whereof ye heard before in the word of the truth of the gospel.

DAY 3

Romans 10:8b–9, 17: The word is nigh thee, even in thy mouth, and in thy heart: that is, the word of faith, which we preach; That if thou shalt confess with thy mouth the Lord Jesus, and shalt believe in thine heart that God hath raised him from the dead, thou shalt be saved. . . So then faith cometh by hearing, and hearing by the word of God.

DAY 4

Hebrews 11:1–2: Now faith is the substance of things hoped for, the evidence of things not seen. For by it the elders obtained a good report.

DAY 5

John 2:11: This beginning of miracles did Jesus in Cana of Galilee, and manifested forth his glory; and his disciples believed on him.

DAY 6

Romans 1:16: For I am not ashamed of the gospel of Christ: for it is the power of God unto salvation to every one that believeth; to the Jew first, and also to the Greek.

DAY 7

Matthew 17:19–20: Then came the disciples to Jesus apart, and said, Why could not we cast him out? And Jesus said unto them, Because of your unbelief: for verily I say unto you, If ye have faith as a grain of mustard seed, ye shall say unto this mountain, Remove hence to yonder place; and it shall remove; and nothing shall be impossible unto you.

DAY 8

Matthew 8:8, 10: The centurion answered and said, Lord, I am not worthy that thou shouldest come under my roof: but speak the word only, and my servant shall be healed . . . When Jesus heard it, he marvelled, and said to them that followed, Verily I say unto you, I have not found so great faith, no, not in Israel.

DAY 9

Matthew 14:25b—31: Jesus went unto them, walking on the sea. And when the disciples saw him walking on the sea, they were troubled, saying, It is a spirit; and they cried out for fear. But straightway Jesus spake unto them, saying, Be of good cheer; it is I; be not afraid. And Peter answered him and said, Lord, if it be thou, bid me come unto thee on the water. And he said, Come. And when Peter was come down out of the ship, he walked on the water, to go to Jesus. But when he saw the wind boisterous, he was afraid; and beginning to sink, he cried, saying, Lord, save me. And immediately Jesus stretched forth his hand, and caught him, and said unto him, O thou of little faith, wherefore didst thou doubt?

DAY 10

Matthew 21:21–22: Jesus answered and said unto them, Verily I say unto you, If ye have faith, and doubt not, ye shall not only do this which is done to the fig tree, but also if ye shall say unto this mountain, Be thou removed, and be thou cast into the sea; it shall be done. And all things, whatsoever ye shall ask in prayer, believing, ye shall receive.

DAY 11

Luke 5:18–25: And, behold, men brought in a bed a man which was taken with a palsy: and they sought means to bring him in, and to lay him before him. And when they could not find by what way they might bring him in because of the multitude, they went upon the housetop, and let him down through the tiling with his couch into the midst before Jesus. And when he saw their faith, he said unto him, Man, thy sins are forgiven thee. . . . I say unto thee, Arise, and take up thy couch, and go into thine house. And immediately he rose up before them, and took up that whereon he lay, and departed to his own house, glorifying God.

DAY 12

Luke 22:31–32: Simon, Simon, behold, Satan hath desired to have you, that he may sift you as wheat: But I have prayed for thee, that thy faith fail not: and when thou art converted, strengthen thy brethren.

DAY 13

Romans 4:1–3: What shall we say then that Abraham our father, as pertaining to the flesh, hath found? For if Abraham were justified by works, he hath whereof to glory; but not before God. For what saith the scripture? Abraham believed God, and it was counted unto him for righteousness.

DAY 14

Galatians 2:20: I am crucified with Christ: nevertheless I live; yet not I, but Christ liveth in me: and the life which I now live in the flesh I live by the faith of the Son of God, who loved me, and gave himself for me.

DAY 15

Romans 8:24–25: For we are saved by hope: but hope that is seen is not hope: for what a man seeth, why doth he yet hope for? But if we hope for that we see not, then do we with patience wait for it.

DAY 16

Romans 15:13: Now the God of hope fill you with all joy and peace in believing, that ye may abound in hope, through the power of the Holy Ghost.

DAY 17

1 Timothy 4:9–10: This is a faithful saying and worthy of all acceptation. For therefore we both labour and suffer reproach, because we trust in the living God, who is the Saviour of all men, specially of those that believe.

DAY 18

2 Corinthians 1:8b–11a: . . . we were pressed out of measure, above strength, insomuch that we despaired even of life: Who delivered us from so great a death, and doth deliver: in whom we trust that he will yet deliver us; Ye also helping together by prayer for us . . .

DAY 19

Romans 5:1–5: Therefore being justified by faith, we have peace with God through our Lord Jesus Christ: By whom also we have access by faith into this grace wherein we stand, and rejoice in hope of the glory of God. And not only so, but we glory in tribulations also: knowing that tribulation worketh patience; And patience, experience; and experience, hope: father of many nations, according to that which was spoken, So shall thy seed be. And hope maketh not ashamed; because the love of God is shed abroad in our hearts by the Holy Ghost which is given unto us.

DAY 20

Romans 4:16b–18: . . . to the end the promise might be sure to all the seed; not to that only which is of the law, but to that also which is of the faith of Abraham; who is the father of us all, (As it is written, I have made thee a father of many nations,) before him whom he believed, even God, who quickeneth the dead, and calleth those things which be not as though they were. Who against hope believed in hope, that he might become the father of many nations, according to that which was spoken, So shall thy seed be.

DAY 21

2 Thessalonians 2:16–17: Now our Lord Jesus Christ himself, and God, even our Father, which hath loved us, and hath given us everlasting consolation and good hope through grace, Comfort your hearts, and stablish you in every good word and work.

DAY 22

Hebrews 6:19–20: Which hope we have as an anchor of the soul, both sure and stedfast, and which entereth into that within the veil; Whither the forerunner is for us entered, even Jesus, made an high priest for ever after the order of Melchisedec.

DAY 23

1 Peter 3:15–16: But sanctify the Lord God in your hearts: and be ready always to give an answer to every man that asketh you a reason of the hope that is in you with meekness and fear: Having a good conscience; that, whereas they speak evil of you, as of evildoers, they may be ashamed that falsely accuse your good conversation in Christ.

DAY 24

1 John 3:1–3: Behold, what manner of love the Father hath bestowed upon us, that we should be called the sons of God: therefore the world knoweth us not, because it knew him not. Beloved, now are we the sons of God, and it doth not yet appear what we shall be: but we know that, when he shall appear, we shall be like him; for we shall see him as he is. And every man that hath this hope in him purifieth himself, even as he is pure.

DAY 25

1 Peter 1:3–6: Blessed be the God and Father of our Lord Jesus Christ, which according to his abundant mercy hath begotten us again unto a lively hope by the resurrection of Jesus Christ from the dead, To an inheritance incorruptible, and undefiled, and that fadeth not away, reserved in heaven for you, Who are kept by the power of God through faith unto salvation ready to be revealed in the last time. Wherein ye greatly rejoice, though now for a season, if need be, ye are in heaviness through manifold temptations.

DAY 26

1 Corinthians 15:19–20: If in this life only we have hope in Christ, we are of all men most miserable. But now is Christ risen from the dead, and become the firstfruits of them that slept.

DAY 27

1 John 4:7–11: Beloved, let us love one another: for love is of God; and every one that loveth is born of God, and knoweth God. He that loveth not knoweth not God; for God is love. In this was manifested the love of God toward us, because that God sent his only begotten Son into the world, that we might live through him. Herein is love, not that we loved God, but that he loved us, and sent his Son to be the propitiation for our sins. Beloved, if God so loved us, we ought also to love one another.

DAY 28

John 15:1, 4–5: I am the true vine, and my Father is the husbandman . . . Abide in me, and I in you. As the branch cannot bear fruit of itself, except it abide in the vine; no more can ye, except ye abide in me. I am the vine, ye are the branches: He that abideth in me, and I in him, the same bringeth forth much fruit: for without me ye can do nothing.

DAY 29

John 3:16–18: For God so loved the world, that he gave his only begotten Son, that whosoever believeth in him should not perish, but have everlasting life. For God sent not his Son into the world to condemn the world; but that the world through him might be saved. He that believeth on him is not condemned: but he that believeth not is condemned already, because he hath not believed in the name of the only begotten Son of God.

DAY 30

John 13:1: Now before the feast of the passover, when Jesus knew that his hour was come that he should depart out of this world unto the Father, having loved his own which were in the world, he loved them unto the end.

DAY 31

John 13:34–35: A new commandment I give unto you, That ye love one another; as I have loved you, that ye also love one another. By this shall all men know that ye are my disciples, if ye have love one to another.

DAY 32

Matthew 5:43–48: Ye have heard that it hath been said, Thou shalt love thy neighbour, and hate thine enemy. But I say unto you, Love your enemies, bless them that curse you, do good to them that hate you, and pray for them which despitefully use you, and persecute you; That ye may be the children of your Father which is in heaven: for he maketh his sun to rise on the evil and on the good, and sendeth rain on the just and on the unjust. For if ye love them which love you, what reward have ye? do not even the publicans the same? And if ye salute your brethren only, what do ye more than others? do not even the publicans so? Be ye therefore perfect, even as your Father which is in heaven is perfect.

DAY 33

Matthew 22:36–40: Master, which is the great commandment in the law? Jesus said unto him, Thou shalt love the Lord thy God with all thy heart, and with all thy soul, and with all thy mind. This is the first and great commandment. And the second is like unto it, Thou shalt love thy neighbour as thyself. On these two commandments hang all the law and the prophets.

DAY 34

Romans 13:8–9: Owe no man any thing, but to love one another: for he that loveth another hath fulfilled the law. For this, Thou shalt not commit adultery, Thou shalt not kill, Thou shalt not steal, Thou shalt not bear false witness, Thou shalt not covet; and if there be any other commandment, it is briefly comprehended in this saying, namely, Thou shalt love thy neighbour as thyself.

DAY 35

1 Peter 4:8: And above all things have fervent charity among yourselves: for charity shall cover the multitude of sins.

DAY 36

Ephesians 4:14–16: That we henceforth be no more children, tossed to and fro, and carried about with every wind of doctrine, by the sleight of men, and cunning craftiness, whereby they lie in wait to deceive; But speaking the truth in love, may grow up into him in all things, which is the head, even Christ: From whom the whole body fitly joined together and compacted by that which every joint supplieth, according to the effectual working in the measure of every part, maketh increase of the body unto the edifying of itself in love.

DAY 37

Ephesians 3:17b–19: That ye, being rooted and grounded in love, May be able to comprehend with all saints what is the breadth, and length, and God.

DAY 38

1 Corinthians 13:4–8a: Charity suffereth long, and is kind; charity envieth not; charity vaunteth not itself, is not puffed up, Doth not behave itself unseemly, seeketh not her own, is not easily provoked, thinketh no evil; Rejoiceth not in iniquity, but rejoiceth in the truth; Beareth all things, believeth all things, hopeth all things, endureth all things. Charity never faileth.

DAY 39

1 Thessalonians 1:2–3: We give thanks to God always for you all, making mention of you in our prayers; Remembering without ceasing your work of faith, and labour of love, and patience of hope in our Lord Jesus Christ, in the sight of God and our Father.

DAY 40

1 Thessalonians 5:7–9: For they that sleep sleep in the night; and they that be drunken are drunken in the night. But let us, who are of the day, be sober, putting on the breastplate of faith and love; and for an helmet, the hope of salvation. For God hath not appointed us to wrath, but to obtain salvation by our Lord Jesus Christ.

ACKNOWLEDGMENTS

The completion of this book, the final product of years of reflection and planning, could not have been possible without several key people. The proofing and suggestions of my wife Sue were helpful throughout. Another level of review by several others was invaluable in the corrections, revisions, and editing of the draft manuscript. The help from my daughter Cheryl Puite, my friends Dr. Dwight and Vangie Jaggard, Rev. Keith and Marti Tanis, relatives Jack and Ginny Kramer, and John and Marge Kuiper were of great help and encouragement.

After forty years of full-time ministry as a pastor and chaplain, and now continuing part-time work as a hospice chaplain, I have learned from so many of God's people whom I had the privilege to serve. Their stories and our reciprocal service to one another underlie many of the insights written. These life experiences together with the wonderful foundations given in my higher education at Calvin University and Calvin Theological Seminary in Grand Rapids, Michigan, have all been a gift which has enabled me to put together these devotions which I hope will bless many of God's struggling people on their pilgrimage.

Last, but not least, the essential skills and help I needed to complete this has come through the advice and work of my capable copy editor, Ann E. Byle, and the wise and patient navigation through the mysteries of the publishing process from my publisher, Timothy Beals of Credo House Publishers. I am truly indebted to them for their service to me!